Items should be returned on or before the last date shown below. Items not already requested by other borrowers may be renewed in person, in writing or by telephone. To renew, please quote the number on the barcode label. To renew online a PIN is required. This can be requested at your local library.
Renew online @ **www.dublincitypubliclibraries.ie**
Fines charged for overdue items will include postage incurred in recovery. Damage to or loss of items will be charged to the borrower.

Leabharlanna Poiblí Chathair Bhaile Átha Cliath
Dublin City Public Libraries

Baile Átha Cliath
Dublin City

An Leabharlann, Sráid Annraoi
Tel: 8734333

Date Due	Date Due	Date Due

D1349985

Do Parents Matter?

Why Japanese Babies Sleep Soundly,
Mexican Siblings Don't Fight, *and*
Parents Should Just Relax

Robert A. LeVine *and*
Sarah LeVine

Souvenir Press

For Bella, Rosie, and Eva

Contents

We the Parents: A Worldwide Perspective

IN 1969, RECENTLY married but not yet parents, we went to a small Nigerian town in the Sahel region south of the Sahara Desert in West Africa on our first field project together. Our goals were to discover how the Hausa people raised their children and to compare their parenting practices with those of America and Europe, beginning with infant care and the social attachment of infants to their mothers.

The Hausa are West Africa's largest ethnic group.[1] Most are Muslims, but they share many family life and child care customs with other West African peoples regardless of religion: polygamy, early marriage for girls, high rates of divorce, child fostering and adoption, and kin-avoidance practices (rules forbidding certain types of social contact within the family). Over seven months, Sarah was welcomed into dozens of households of women secluded from men (including Bob) to talk with mothers and grandmothers and observe babies and young children. Her experience raised questions about what constitutes adequate infant care, questions that remain with us today.

The Hausa code of kin-avoidance is called *kunya*. It forbids a woman to utter her husband's name or to speak to her oldest child (and in many cases her younger children too) or engage him or her in eye contact, even in infancy. While many other African peoples also practice kin-avoidance, the version Sarah encountered among Hausa-Fulani families was among the most restrictive on the African continent.[2]

Sarah met fifteen-year-old Rabi, who had given birth to Amina, her first child, in her husband's home. Rabi had brought her four-month-old infant daughter to her parents' house for an extended visit. During the half-hour Sarah spent in the house one morning, Rabi's mother, Delu, held her plump, bright-eyed granddaughter Amina on her lap. But Rabi, who was sitting about a yard away, didn't look at or speak to the baby. Every so often a group of children would run up, play with Amina's fingers and toes, make her laugh, and run away. Deserted, Amina would start to cry, prompting the grandmother to hand her to Rabi, who would nurse her, stony-faced.

Anthropologists are expected to cultivate objectivity, but while Sarah tried to do so, her training as a psychiatric social worker and child therapist deepened her dismay at what she regarded as Rabi's unnatural behavior. She had been taught that a mother's lack of warmth for her baby would do drastic harm to the infant's psyche. Sarah only began to question that assumption when she met an exceptionally bright and engaging Hausa university student named Musa. A chief's son and the oldest child of his mother, he had experienced kin-avoidance as an infant. Furthermore, like many other Hausa children, he had been sent after weaning in the second year of his life to a cousin in a distant district and had not been reunited with his biological parents until he was fifteen years old. How could this young man, who would later earn a PhD in the United States and become a senior

Nigerian government official, have come through these "adverse" experiences with no apparent damage to his mental health? His case and others among the Hausa seemed to challenge the most authoritative Western thinking of the time on infant development. In this book, we consider many such challenges from all over the known world of Asia, Africa, Europe, Latin America, and the Pacific. We also set contemporary variations in parental ideas and practices in a historical perspective. Over the last 3,000 years, the standards for parenting were shaped by humankind's reliance on family-based agriculture and animal husbandry. But since 1800, and particularly in the early twentieth century, lifestyles in the developed (urban-industrial and postindustrial) countries and, more recently, in some of the less developed (poorer, agrarian) countries have changed how we parent. Since 90 percent of the world's children are currently being raised in the agrarian countries, we consider the questions that their practices raise for American parents.

If American parents knew more about child-rearing elsewhere in the world, they might have a better chance of evaluating, and perhaps resisting, advice directed to them from the media, the Internet, and the "experts." Margaret Mead made this point in her classic *Growing Up in New Guinea* in 1930, arguing that cross-cultural diversity in parenting is like an experiment: we can benefit from the experience of parents elsewhere before trying new practices ourselves.[3] She initiated the project of recording parental experience in other cultures, a project in which we have participated for much of our lives, working in Africa, Latin America, and South Asia. In this book, we draw upon our observations and those of other anthropologists and child psychologists, comparing American parents with parents from all over the world.

As evidence on parenting in different cultures has accumulated over the eighty-six years since Margaret Mead published

Growing Up in New Guinea, we have lost her confidence that reading the answers presented in the ways of life of different peoples is simple or straightforward. There have been too many hasty judgments of the parental practices of other peoples, ranging from condemnation to admiration. We need to examine those practices in greater depth, from a child development perspective, and particularly from the viewpoints of the parents in their cultures and ours.

A few years back a group of behavioral scientists openly recognized what anthropologists have been saying since Margaret Mead: that what passes for general knowledge in psychology is based largely on studies of individuals from Western, Educated, Industrialized, Rich, and Democratic (WEIRD) societies.[4] In social psychology, the subjects are mostly college sophomores at American universities. In child psychology, despite serious efforts to broaden the scope of research, many theorists still feel free to generalize about human development from local samples in the United States that are unrepresentative of—indeed outliers in— the human species. We now know that children are raised under a wide range of conditions and that human parents approach reproduction, infant care, and the rearing of toddlers and older children in diverse ways, many of them discussed in this book.

Transforming Parenthood

Parenting has undergone three major transformations in human history. The first began with the invention of agriculture and animal husbandry 11,000 years ago. As food production gradually spread, parents became supervisors of their children's work in a home production team. A majority of humans lived this way, under varied agrarian conditions, for at least 3,000 years; for them, obedience to parents was a sacred virtue. Then, about 250 years ago, the second transformation began as industrial production drew families into cities with factories, markets, and state bureaucracies and productive work moved out of the home. In the twentieth century, bureaucratic health care systems were established, children were sent to school, and family incomes increased. This second transformation is still under way; the world's urban population moved past the 50 percent mark for the first time in 2007.

A third, and concurrent, transformation in parenting known as the "demographic transition" occurred during the twentieth century, when medical and socioeconomic advances brought down infant and child mortality rates and then fertility rates, first in Western countries and East Asia and eventually in most of the world, to low levels hardly imagined as recently as 1900.

At the present time, there is a great divide between the wealthiest and most developed countries (in North America, Europe, and East Asia) and the low-income countries in Africa, Asia, and Latin America, which have more than twelve times the under-five mortality of high-income countries and almost twice the fertility. Ninety percent of the world's children are being raised in these agrarian and transitional countries. The trend toward modern conditions is unmistakable everywhere, but there are still many societies where child mortality rates are high, children are numerous, and they work for their parents. On the other side of the divide, modern parents enjoy the unprecedented assurance that hardly any of their few children will die and none will have to work during childhood, yet they are remarkably anxious about the risks their offspring face—far more than the parents we have worked with in other, less fortunate, societies.

It is tempting to use simple dichotomies like rich versus poor, agrarian versus modern, and collectivist versus individualist to explain the diversity of parenting across the globe. However, parenting cannot be fully understood in those terms. Parents in every society have a distinctive cultural heritage of child-rearing ideas and practices they adapt to the local situations they experience in their own generation, and that creates differences in parenting from one agrarian people to another as well as among the modern societies of the world. For most parents, it is hard to imagine ways of child-rearing other than those that are conventional in their communities. They are amazed, sometimes outraged, that anybody could do things differently. Here are some parenting practices and their reflections in early child behavior that vary more widely than many American parents might imagine.

Fear Versus Sociability: African Toddlers' Reaction to Strangers

Let's start with fear or friendliness as reactions to a strange-looking anthropologist. When Bob first walked through a rural (Gusii) community in Kenya in the 1950s, toddlers fled from his path, some of them screaming in fear, a reaction they gradually relinquished as he became a familiar figure there. But when he first visited a Yoruba neighborhood in the city of Ibadan, Nigeria, a few years later, children of the same age greeted him boldly in cheerful, giggling groups, hugged his legs, dogged his steps, and could not be discouraged from their extreme friendliness, though they were no more accustomed to white visitors than their Kenyan counterparts. How is it that the reactions of children to an odd visitor had become so different in these two populations by the time they were about three years old or even younger? The answer had to be in their prior social experience, perhaps taking place as early as infancy.

The living arrangements in which Gusii and Yoruba infants were raised seemed to tell part of the story: young children lived with their mothers in both societies, but a Gusii mother and her children occupied a separate hut with its own front yard, where other adults and children came only as occasional visitors, whereas the Yoruba mothers lived in a bustling compound sharing hearth, yard, and veranda with other mothers and children and having frequent encounters with visitors. In other words, Yoruba domestic social life was much greater in sheer density than that of the Gusii, and the Yoruba child grew up associating with many more people, strangers as well as kin, of all ages. Furthermore, although infant care by older siblings or other children was known in both communities, Yoruba babies were more frequently cared for by adult women—grandmothers, childless aunts, and older women living in the compound. Thus, the relative isolation of the Gusii children compared with their Yoruba counterparts seemed to account for their greater wariness and fear of strange adults.

An equally important part of the story, however, was the invisible environment of cultural ideals. For Yoruba adults, the prevailing ideal was one of sociability and gregariousness; in this environment, extended greetings, cheerful and noisy interaction, lengthy and hilarious conversations, and expressions of concern for the welfare of others were mandatory as well as commonplace. No child could escape this kind of upbeat interpersonal performance, and all would begin to learn the script. The Gusii, however, were reticent about interpersonal encounters outside the domestic group, believing excessive sociability to be dangerous for a person of any age, and their conversational interaction was governed by a code of restraint. Even young children were warned against too much mingling with strangers.[5] Parents told us they wanted their children to learn fear.

Thus, two agrarian peoples in Africa diverge in something so fundamental to raising children as how they should behave toward adults, including strangers, and, more broadly, whether to encourage or discourage sociability in children.

Modern societies show similar contrasts. The Japanese and Chinese are neighbors in East Asia, share a great deal of cultural background and history, and are both often categorized as "collectivist" or "interdependent" in comparison with "individualist" Westerners. Why, then, wouldn't they resemble each other in parenting? In fact, however, there are dramatic differences between them in the ideals that guide the parenting of toddlers, even among urban middle-class families in contemporary Japan and (Chinese) Taiwan, despite their common concern about their children's future academic success. This is transparently clear in video observations of parents with young children made by Shusuke Kobayashi in Japan and Heidi Fung and her team in Taiwan.[6]

Patience Versus Confrontation in Mothering

Kobayashi, then a young graduate student at Harvard, gained access to private homes in Japan by seeking the cooperation of ten mothers he had known in school. They welcomed him into their apartments to video their two- to three-year-olds at snack time. He found, and his videos show, that as mothers tried, sometimes desperately, to teach their children table manners—for example, to not throw food on the floor—they avoided chastising their little trainees, no matter how much the toddlers tried their patience. It is amazing to an American viewer of his videos that they could maintain their sweet and upbeat attitude in the face of persistent misbehavior. Softening their commands as questions or hints, they refrained from using the imperative but never gave up on attempting to secure the child's cooperation.

You might think that these mothers were exceptionally—from a Western point of view, almost comically—patient individuals, but they were following a standard Japanese cultural model of learning that is intended to protect the teacher-learner relationship as a positive emotional bond first and foremost in order to ensure that learning occurs. Japanese believe that scolding and other forms of confrontation will jeopardize the "sticky" (that is, adhesive) relationship that in the long run will achieve the teacher's goals. These sweet but persistent mothers were able to outlast their young children's resistance without losing that nonconfrontational style. They may have seemed to an American observer to be "coddling" or "indulging" their toddlers, but they were pursuing a strategy that would result in training them.

In Taiwan, Heidi Fung, an established researcher trained at the University of Chicago and based at the highly respected Academia Sinica in Taipei, also videotaped middle-class mothers at home with their two- to three-year-olds. These mothers, unlike their Japanese counterparts, *sought* confrontations with their young children over current or even remembered instances of misbehavior. They were following a traditional Chinese script for "opportunity education" (*jihui jiaoyu*), in which parents take advantage of a misdeed, either one that has just occurred or one referred to in conversation, to chastise the child and deliver explicit instruction on proper behavior and moral virtue. The Taiwanese mothers believed—contrary to their Japanese counterparts—that these confrontations and moral lectures would build rather than destroy their learning relationship with their child; for their part, the young children in Taiwan were not necessarily upset at having their transgressions exposed in the presence of the investigator or even at being harangued by their mothers. In the videos, they do not seem anxious about their mothers' approval, and they appear to regard the moral lectures as familiar experiences. It is evident that the Japanese mothers who avoided confrontation with their toddlers and the Chinese mothers who sought it represent different premises about how to raise a child.

Parents have different goals depending on their cultural traditions. In an agrarian setting, parents' emphasis on hierarchy, obedience, and fertility is rooted in and reinforced by the household economy, but as the Gusii-Yoruba contrast suggests, there are different ways of being agrarian. And the contrast between Japanese and Chinese mothers shows that modern, urban mothers are similarly varied. Parents are not immune to adaptive pressures, and their practices change from generation to generation, reflecting their changing environments. But they are not simply rational decision-makers: their child-rearing ideas and practices are infused with the moral ideas of a particular tradition.

Variability

The world of parenting encompasses wide variations that seem bewildering, though that world is no more varied than the plants and animals Darwin first encountered—and the variations occur within a single species under increasingly well-documented conditions. Anyone expecting to find a fixed or universal system of parental behavior for the entire species would certainly be disappointed. For example, even African hunter-gatherers—once assumed to be survivors of a single ancestral population from which we are all descended—vary widely in infant care: !Kung San mothers of the Kalahari Desert care for their babies largely by themselves; mothers among the Efe of the Ituri forest share the care, including breast-feeding, with other women in the same camp; and among the Aka of the northern Congo rain forest, fathers play a major role in infant care, more than has ever been documented for any other population. Each parenting pattern makes sense in terms of the hunting and gathering practices on which the group depends for food, but the variation is striking for these peoples as for others.

In the agrarian world, there is wide variation on every social factor imaginable: marriage, divorce, household size, formality of interaction at home, the position of women. Polygamy is standard in most African societies, but its frequency and the relations of the co-wives vary greatly; in the rest of the world polygamy is illegal, as in our own society, or restricted to four wives, as in Islamic societies, or limited to secret unions, as in Mexico (the *casa chica*). Legal marriage is going out of style in western Europe, and it's been a rarity for a long while in the West Indies, but it's still the major focus of social life in India. Divorce is rare in India and elsewhere in South Asia, but very frequent in West Africa, where many women as well as men marry several times. The Indian joint family is large—there were 25 million male-headed households with seven or more persons living in them in the 2011 census of India—but in East Africa each mother tends to live in a house just with her own children. We found the domestic behavior of Africans and Asians to be highly scripted, especially according to respect in a hierarchical family, in striking contrast to the informality of American parents and their children at home. Women are subordinated in many families of Africa and India, where they may also be regarded as polluted, but far less so in the Southeast Asian societies of Thailand, the Philippines, and Indonesia, where something closer to gender equality prevails.

This variability in social conditions—and the rules and codes of family behavior in particular communities—reduces the scope of personal choice even in America, where we like to think we can decide how to be a parent. The fact is that we too are standardized in the marital and household arrangements in which we raise our children. We tend to conform to the recognized standards of our own class, community, generation, and friendship circle.

Morality

The moral force of child-rearing codes becomes clear when one travels across cultural boundaries. In 1497 the ambassador of Venice to the court of King Henry VII of England wrote a letter home describing the English "want of affection," as manifested in their sending their children out to be apprentices in other families' homes, a practice he termed "repulsive."[7] Five hundred years later, in 1997, the New York City police arrested a Danish mother for parking her baby in a carriage *outside* the restaurant in which she and the baby's father were eating, a practice she claimed—correctly—was customary at home in Copenhagen. And in the German-speaking countries of Europe, at least before 1980, it was common practice for mothers to leave babies and toddlers alone at home in their cribs while they went shopping in the daytime or attended a party with their husbands at night. This would have been legally punishable as neglect in the United States at the time, and in fact European tourists and immigrants in the United States have been reported to the police by neighbors when they hear a child crying. Moral and legal standards vary, and the emotions supporting them run high.

These variations show us that what is standard in the treatment of children in one society may be unacceptable, illegal, or "abnormal" in another. The wide array of "normal" child-rearing patterns in the world may challenge the advice of American experts and raise new questions about how much parents influence their children. Have American parents been misled by experts about the psychological impact of what they do and its risk of damaging their children?

Psychiatry?

We need first of all to free our thinking about parental influence from the psychiatric perspective in which parenting is defined by its potential to make children mentally ill. Parental practices vary much too widely across cultures for us to accept uncritically the supposition that the mental health of American children is being put at risk by "insensitive" infant care. The resilience of children under varied conditions is far more evident than the emotional vulnerability in which many American parents believe.

As we show in Chapter 1, experts in pediatrics, public health, and psychiatry have provided advice that claimed the authority of science while blending moral ideology with empirical evidence. In retrospect, the unscientific nature of much of this expert advice, despite its empirical contents, casts doubt on the notion of parenting as science. There may be a science of parenting one day, but premature attempts to build a general theory of human parenting have tended to oversimplify the evidence, ignore exceptions, and use fallacious analogies about adaptation or progress.

Modern parents in America and elsewhere seek to optimize their children's life chances and exert a virtuous influence on their children's development. But the expert advice that parents attend to has grossly exaggerated the influence of parenting on child development, inflating its predictability beyond the evidence and underestimating the resilience of children and the likelihood of change in later childhood and adolescence. The time has come for American parents to reconsider the burdens they place on themselves, for dubious ends.

When we were new parents in Chicago in the early 1970s, we practiced a version of the child-centered style of parenting, which seemed to come naturally to us, though we were not ourselves raised that way. Indeed, our own early childhood experiences were sharply different: Bob, an only child raised in a small Manhattan apartment, had early memories of his rather strict mother and playing by himself in his room and the park; Sarah, the second of three siblings, was raised in an English manor house and had memories of her uniformed nanny and her siblings but none of her parents. When we ourselves became parents, we were probably as enthusiastic about every one of our children's advances in motor development or language—praising, cheering, taking pictures or home movies—as any other American parents at the time. We always responded to their solicitations of our attention and often let them interrupt adult conversations. And we were quick to prop them up with encouragement should their spirits falter. In these respects, we behaved differently from the way our far more restrained and distant parents—or the servants who cared for Sarah and her younger brother—had behaved in the 1930s and 1940s.

Sarah remembers the day's schedule as set in stone. It centered on meals (in the "day nursery"): breakfast, "elevenses" (snack), lunch, "high tea," and bed at seven o'clock in the "night nursery," which she shared with her brother and "nursie" (who had also raised their considerably older sister). There was a lot of playing, being read to, and being taken for walks; long after napping was a thing of the past there was an obligatory rest in the afternoon. After Sarah's fifth birthday, for which she received her first pony, learning to ride was added to the schedule. Before she and her brother went to kindergarten, the objective was to keep them calm and busy until they had learned to read, at which point books would take the place of physical activity. Companionship was provided by the servants, who were numerous, attentive, and unfailingly kind. Adult expectations were clear: being "naughty" and "showing off" were frowned upon.

Sarah remembers feeling safe, cared for, and—fairly often— bored as a child. When she became a mother, she soon began to notice that she was more structured and stricter with her children than her Chicago friends were with theirs, particularly about bedtimes. For though she saw the shortcomings of the way she had been brought up, she also saw its benefits. Like Bob, she was all for letting children "unfold like flowers," but within limits. American hyper-individualism scared her!

We nevertheless adopted the new child-centered style of parenting, though not based on a conscious calculation that it would improve Anna's and Alex's life chances. Rather, our behavior with the children felt consistent with the people we had become, expressing an identity that belonged to us in particular as well as to our generation. We were, in short, reflecting a shift in American (and British) child-rearing that had already been under way for some two or three decades.

Child-rearing practices, styles, and codes have continued to change since we were new parents in the 1970s. More mothers work, more infants and toddlers are cared for outside the home, and there is far more concern about risks, even for older children, than was true in those days. Parenting for middle-class Americans (the educated middle class, as opposed to working-class, blue-collar, or poor) has become more labor-intensive and stressful, as the sociologist Annette Lareau and the journalist Jennifer Senior have documented in detail, and as we discuss in the final chapter.[8]

Learning about the worldwide cultural variations in child-rearing practices reviewed in this book will not answer all your questions about parenting, but it may well change how you think about your own parenting practices—not by raising your anxiety about the choices you've made, but by giving you a fresh view of them in the wider context of human parenting as a whole.

Parent-Blaming in America

IN THIS BOOK we propose a new way of thinking about how parents affect their children's development—one that is social as well as psychological, consistent with the cross-cultural evidence, and less worrisome for parents than the views that have been dominant for many years. Theories offered as scientific have grossly exaggerated not only the amount of parents' psychological influence but also the risks that parents face in raising their children.

We see parents as their children's *sponsors* in a social world with multiple influences, setting priorities for the training of young children and selecting the environments that will shape their children's development rather than influencing that development themselves. This viewpoint retreats from the exorbitant claims of psychological influence that were prominent in public discourse about parenting during the middle decades of the twentieth century and have never been fully dispelled.

During that period, psychiatrists and psychoanalysts replaced pediatricians as advice-givers and captured public attention through best-selling books and magazine articles that blamed parents for their children's mental disorders. Psychiatrists or psychoanalysts serving as advice-givers to parents differ drastically from pediatricians like Benjamin Spock. Pediatricians, whatever their prejudices, are general practitioners who work with and monitor basically healthy children as they undergo minor and major illnesses. Child psychiatrists and psychoanalysts, however, are specialists who see *only* those children already considered problematic in their behavior by parents or teachers. Psychoanalysts treating adults are even further removed from ordinary children, being exposed primarily to their patients' childhood memories. Thus, when these mental health practitioners formulate the advice they would give to the ordinary parent, they have to *imagine* what normal child development is like, without basing it directly on their own experience as practitioners. They may draw on their personal experience as parents or on their construction of an ideal child who lacks the pathologies they confront in their practice. We believe that they almost always *under*estimate the variability of child behaviors accepted as normal in the general population. In effect, mental health professionals treat "normal" as a coherent "syndrome" similar to a diagnostic category of disease in medicine, marked by a certain set of tendencies and attitudes. But "normal" behavior is actually a broad range of (nonpathological) behaviors and dispositions; there are many kinds of normal. As a result, experts end up putting pathological labels on a large part of that normal range, thus exaggerating the dangers of "abnormal" development. Where did these exaggerations come from, and how did they come to be believed?

Public Responsibility: The Government and Parents

In the early years of the republic, the US population was largely rural, parents were responsible for their own children, and the

Protestant churches provided moral guidance and schools in which a majority of boys, and a lesser proportion of girls, acquired biblical literacy. In the mid-nineteenth century, this began to change as mass public schooling became established and, together with urbanization, immigration, industrialization, and new conceptions of the child, altered the conditions for parenting.

One early landmark is the Massachusetts legislature's adoption of the "Prussian system of education" in 1852, on the recommendation of the state's secretary of education, Horace Mann, who had visited schools in Prussia, England, and Scotland in 1843.[1] This was a *secular* system of public schools offering *standardized* instruction to *all* children, with a bureaucratic organization designed to maintain quality and equality through inspection, examinations, and teacher training. Mann promoted its spread throughout the United States, and it became the form that spread to many other countries as well. Public school education did not become universal in the United States immediately, but it expanded rapidly after the end of the Civil War in 1865, and by the end of the century primary schooling was virtually universal.

When the various US states passed laws to make schooling compulsory (as most European countries also did, at the national level, in the 1870s), thus requiring parents to send their children to school, they were assuming a responsibility that had previously belonged to parents. But the rise of public responsibility for children did not end there. Americans, like the British Victorian-era reformers before them, increasingly recognized that children were being abandoned, exploited, and abused under conditions wrought by urbanization and industrialization. Influenced by representations of children as innocent victims in Romantic literature (notably, the novels of Charles Dickens), they sought remedies in political and social action. The sentimental conception of the child in literature was a call to action in the real world and gave rise to organized reform movements. The New York Society for the Prevention of Cruelty to Children was founded in 1875, followed by the Massachusetts society of the same name three years later, and orphanages were established to provide care to those who had lost their parents.

The number of adults infused with a concern for *other people's children* kept growing, and with it the sense that society and its representatives in government must intervene with laws and institutions to protect innocent children from exploitation and other harsh conditions. The political struggle against child labor began in this period and continued into the twentieth century. Industrialization, with children working in factories and mines, slowed down the expansion of school attendance in some places, but the battle to ban child labor was ultimately won in the twentieth century. The reformers who cared about other people's children established a role for government as the protector—as well as educator—of children, irreversibly modifying the role of parents.

Though public action diminished parents' control over their offspring, the mother's private role as nurturer was idealized in the prevailing spirit of the age. The loving mother was celebrated in romantic paintings, poems, and songs, her domesticity represented in sentimental terms as boundless affection for her infants and toddlers. (Paternal discipline would apply to the older children.) Science had yet to invade the nursery.

Hygiene: Parenting as Disease Prevention

The nineteenth century's educational progress had not been matched by an equivalent improvement in child health. In 1900 the US infant mortality rate (deaths per 1,000 live births in the first year of life) was 100, a rate nowadays considered unacceptable even in the poorest countries. (The current US rate is 6 per 1,000.) Mortality rates of older children and adults were also high. But measures to improve the situation had been made possible by nineteenth-century advances in the scientific understanding of infectious diseases and how to control them. Beginning in the 1890s, state and local governments in the United States undertook major works to improve public health, including sewage disposal systems and the purification of drinking water. The pasteurization of milk followed in the first decades of the twentieth century. Chicago, in 1908, became the first city to pasteurize its milk supply.

In addition to these public health measures, advice to mothers dispensed not only in books and the mass media but also by private charities and governments promoted "hygiene"—the maintenance of sanitary and antiseptic conditions in the home to prevent the transmission of infectious diseases to the young. The care of infants and young children was increasingly seen as a series of medical problems that could be solved through the mother's use of information provided by medical experts.

An influential text in the hygiene movement was *The Care and Feeding of Children: A Catechism for the Use of Mothers and Children's Nurses,* published in 1894 by the New York pediatrician L. Emmett Holt.[2] The book became extremely popular and went through many editions over the next forty years. Set up as a catechism of questions and answers, the book simulates a consultation between a mother and her doctor, but most of the questions are about the routine care of well babies and older children. The answers cover topics ranging from the desirable temperature of the baby's bathwater to the firmness of the child's mattress, with a great deal of attention to diet and food preparation. Holt was a physician, but most of the book is not focused on disease or

pathological conditions; it implicitly asserts his medical expertise as a general warrant for authoritative recommendations on
child care. Some of his admonitions are couched as preventive
medicine: if the mother does not follow his advice, illness could
occur. But some of the advice is designed to provide guidance
in avoiding, or dealing with, "bad habits" and "indulgence," so a
moral element unrelated to hygiene is clearly present. The medical authority of Dr. Holt is extended to include morally correct
training based on a pseudoscientific psychology, as in the following excerpts from the 1914 (seventh) edition:

> *Should a child sleep in the same bed with its mother or nurse?*
> Under no circumstances, if this can possibly be avoided. Very
> young infants have often been smothered by their mothers by
> overlying during sleep. If the infant sleeps with the mother, there
> is always the temptation to frequent nursing at night, which is
> injurious to both mother and child.
> *How is an infant to be managed that cries from temper, habit,
> or to be indulged?*
> It should simply be allowed to "cry it out." This often requires
> an hour, and, in extreme cases, two or three hours.
> *When may young children be played with?*
> If at all, in the morning, or after the mid-day nap; but never
> just before bedtime.
> *Are there any valid objections to kissing infants?*
> There are many serious objections. Tuberculosis, diphtheria,
> syphilis and many other grave diseases may be communicated in
> this way. The kissing of infants upon the mouth by other chil-
> dren, by nurses, or by people generally, should under no circum-
> stances be permitted. Infants should be kissed, if at all, upon the
> cheek or forehead, but the less even of this the better.[3]

The kissing taboo, though weakened in the last statement (Holt often asserts a stern mandate, then qualifies it), is significant culturally because it stands in opposition to the romantic and sentimental mother-child relationship of the mid-nineteenth century, now rejected by a medical expert on a morally higher ground made possible by the scientific understanding of disease transmission. The medical warning also carries with it a moral distaste for the mother's affectionate act. So much for the loving mother!

Holt was helping to usher in a new ideology of parenting, one presented as a scientific concern for the health of the child but carrying with it strong moral overtones censoring affection as a sign of parental weakness and "indulgence" that contributed to the formation of "bad habits" in the child. By 1910, women's magazines were advising mothers, partly reflecting Holt's influence, to feed their infants on a strict schedule, abstain from "love" and physical stimulation, and ignore "unnecessary" crying.[4] And the experts advocated drastic measures for unsanitary habits like thumb-sucking: pediatricians in both Britain and America advised putting splints on toddlers' arms at night.[5] One expert wrote about a remedy for the nail-biting of an older child: "Get some white cotton gloves, and make her wear these all the time—even in school. This will not only serve as a reminder but also make her ashamed when people ask her about them."[6] If these "remedies" seem cruel from our contemporary perspective, they probably did to most parents then too, but they felt helpless in the face of authoritative medical opinion.

This remarkable turn in the ideology of parenting partly reflected the rising prestige of medical doctors. The reform of American medical education had been going on since the late nineteenth century, but it accelerated after 1910, resulting in lengthier, science-based training at medical schools tightly connected to universities and hospitals, the required state certification of doctors, and the closing of many proprietary (local, doctor-owned) medical schools.[7] These measures turned the reduced number of those entitled to call themselves doctors into a professional elite practicing scientific medicine.[8] Even before the reforms, elite pediatricians like Holt were offering their services to affluent mothers (and through charities, to some of the poor) in cities like New York and Baltimore. These women were also among the first readers of Holt's book, but a broader readership for his message of schedules and "no play with baby" would be reached through the women's magazines and, from 1914 to 1921, the widely distributed *Infant Care Bulletins* of the federal government's new Children's Bureau.[9]

Mothers also became increasingly dependent for child-care advice on private consultations with their doctors. Pediatricians and family doctors assumed the role of the family's expert consultant on medical science, a role made possible by the new training for doctors. In the 1930s it was common for middle-class mothers to consult their pediatricians concerning infant and child care, believing, following the Holt model, that their advice represented the latest scientific findings, regardless of whether it was related to disease. Their advice included Holt's strict regimes for feeding, sleeping, and other activities of the infant and young child that were unrelated to hygiene in the narrow sense but presented by the doctor as equally scientific and necessary for health. Mothers felt that they had to obey such orders to maintain a relationship with the doctor, perhaps the only person they ever met who wielded the authority of science—and who made house calls.

In his 1928 book *Psychological Care of Infant and Child* and in the many articles he wrote for popular magazines, John B. Watson declared that scientific child-rearing required parental discipline and emotional restraint during the child's early years.[10] Watson's message was consistent with Holt's, but more aggressively advocated. He was a psychologist and the foremost advocate of behaviorism, an approach exclusively focused on externally observable behavior without speculating about mental processes; behaviorists tend to assume that a child's environment shapes his or her development. Behaviorism does not necessarily favor any particular way of raising children, but Watson claimed that his experiments proved discipline and regimentation to be best. Chapter 3 of his book is titled "The Dangers of Too Much Mother Love." He warns that kissing, coddling, and other expressions of affection will produce children who "are always crying and always whining," which "shows the unhappy, unwholesome state they are in."[11] He advocates treating children like little adults. Despite his claims of scientific validity for this position, it was closer to moral doctrine than to science.

The drastic treatments recommended by experts to parents in the early decades of the twentieth century can be seen as by-products of the first phase of America's great child survival revolution, in which infant mortality declined from 100 per 1,000 in 1900 to 29.2 in 1950; (post-infancy) child mortality showed a similar drop. The hygiene movement had in fact contributed to this improvement. Yet the genuine strides forward in public health and medicine that brought about this unprecedented change were accompanied, especially in doctors' advice to mothers, by a pseudo-scientific ideology of parental discipline and emotional restraint, possibly in opposition to the sentimentality of the previous era. Sentimentality about children had not disappeared, however, as evidenced by the enormously popular Shirley Temple movies of the 1930s. Indeed, the romantic view of children might still have been the most influential child-rearing ideology of the time, but it had yet to find its voice in medical authority. That would happen in the next period.

Mental Health as a Parental Goal

In 1950 the child psychologist Celia Stendler began an article with the following paragraph:

> The past two decades have witnessed a revolution in child training practices in America, which has been tremendous in its scope and far-reaching in its effects. From an era where the mother was taught that the child must have his physical wants cared for and then be left alone, must be fed on a rigid schedule, must learn to cry it out, must be toilet trained early and must not be spoiled by attention, we have come to a time when exactly the opposite advice is advocated. Today the mother is advised to feed the baby when he's hungry, to delay toilet training until he's ready for it, to see that the baby gets a reasonable amount of cuddling and mothering, to let the baby initiate the weaning process. And just as a mother of 1930 was taught that the popular doctrine of that era would produce the right kind of child, so the mother of today is assured that if she weans and toilet trains and cuddles in the approved fashion, her child will have a well-adjusted personality.[12]

Stendler doubted that "the new doctrine is any sounder than the old" and concluded "that the reasons for the revolution lie outside the realm of scientific fact." She traced these trends through a content analysis of three widely read women's magazines, *Ladies' Home Journal, Woman's Home Companion,* and *Good Housekeeping,* from 1890 to 1949. Among her findings were that, while 75 to 100 percent of the articles between 1910 and 1930 advised mothers that infants should be tightly scheduled and learn to "cry it out," only 33 percent did so in 1940, and none did in 1948. She did not explain this trend but noted the growing prominence of the "mental hygiene approach," which began with a series of articles, "Mental Hygiene in the Home," in the *Ladies' Home Journal* in 1930 by Karl Menninger, a Freudian psychoanalyst. (The early date of this series shows how the periods overlapped, with opposing ideologies competing for influence before a new one became dominant.)

The new advice had an effect: surveys during this period showed a distinct trend toward greater permissiveness in the reported behavior of American mothers, beginning in the 1940s, especially among middle-class women—in other words, the mothers who read the magazines and were most attuned to expert advice.[13]

Thus, by 1950 the gospel of preventive medicine through hygiene and rigid scheduling was being replaced by a *mental health ideology* that shifted the focus to children's emotional development. This ideology broadened the concept of mental illness far beyond the severe conditions classified as psychosis that might call for hospitalization to include behaviors and anxieties that could be symptoms of neurosis but were not clearly outside the range of normal behavior. Following Freud's concept of continuity in mental functioning between normal and abnormal, child and adult, sleeping and waking, everyone was potentially subject to the inner conflicts that can lead to mental disorders, but children were especially vulnerable. Parents were accused of jeopardizing their children's long-term mental health, above all by failing to provide the conditions for emotional security in early childhood. As Stendler put it, the "mental hygiene approach to rearing children . . . emphasizes the importance of good emotional health. . . . The child's need for love and affection if he is to be a secure individual is stressed, as is the necessity for understanding the child and accepting him for what he is."[14]

The history of this sea change in concepts of parenting during the middle and second half of the twentieth century has yet to be written, though there have been biographies of its major figures. But having lived through it as participant-observers in the mental health world of that period, we can offer a provisional account of its major currents. We both received training in psychoanalysis, Bob as a research candidate at the Institute for Psychoanalysis in Chicago between 1962 and 1971, Sarah at the University of Chicago, where she studied psychiatric social work from 1964 to 1966. Bob later conducted seminars at the Chicago Institute; Sarah, while undergoing psychoanalysis, practiced psychotherapy at the Jewish Children's Bureau, with Bruno Bettelheim as a consultant. Much later, we taught a seminar together at the Boston Psychoanalytic Society and Institute. Yet our primary commitment was to empirical research, and we were critical of many aspects of psychoanalysis. Our associates over the years have included psychiatrists and social scientists who were leading critics of the ideas of Sigmund Freud as well as those who were advocates.

In considering the mid-twentieth-century shift in views about child-rearing, it must be remembered, first of all, that by 1950 the United States had made great progress as a society in advancing the welfare of children according to Western concepts of human development. There was universal education in the United States, and the length of schooling was being extended; child labor laws were in effect everywhere, and the role of government as protector of children was well established. Infant and child mortality had dramatically declined and was being further reduced through the widespread use of new, effective treatments (especially antibiotics) and immunizations as well as other medical and public health interventions. There was more progress to be made, to be sure, but it was in continuing the advances of earlier periods—extending education for all to high school and college and reducing mortality even further. Thus, parents could feel a measure of confidence in the greatly improved conditions for raising children compared with those of their parents or grandparents. But as this most educated generation of Americans took to the books and magazines for advice about parenting, they were susceptible to new views of what being a good parent meant and what challenges lay ahead in raising children. And they found new causes for concern.

The publication in 1946 of Spock's *Baby and Child Care,* destined to become one of the best-selling books of all time, gave authoritative voice to the trend toward permissiveness that was already under way. For the postwar generation of American mothers, "Dr. Spock," a pediatrician, was a liberator, freeing them from the strictures of previous pediatric advice and encouraging them to depend more on their own judgment in child-rearing, even as they followed his instructions in the book. Spock did not endorse the strict regimes and disciplines of the past as he discussed in detail how a mother might respond to the options and problems presented at each point in her child's development. He wrote: "You hear that a baby is spoiled by being picked up too much, but also that a baby must be cuddled plenty. . . . Don't be overawed by what the experts say. Don't be afraid to trust your own common sense."[15]

Spock may have acquired this empathic attitude in his training at the New York Psychoanalytic Institute, but his advice was not Freudian in content. He stood back from doctrinaire positions on child-rearing as he described changes since the Victorian era, yet he was not neutral: "Doctors who used to conscientiously warn young parents against spoiling are now encouraging them to meet their children's needs, not only for food, but for comforting and loving. These . . . changes of attitudes and methods have benefited most children and parents."[16] His book encouraged discussion among mothers, leading to further questioning, uncertainty, and—inevitably—anxiety about the choices involved. This created a demand for even more expert advice, and now there was a new breed of experts—the psychiatrists and other mental health professionals—ready to satisfy that demand.

The post–World War II period saw an unprecedented expansion of psychiatry and the elevation of its status as a medical specialty as new departments were established in medical schools, more young psychiatrists were trained in federally subsidized hospital residency programs, and greater efforts were made to communicate with the general public. Psychoanalysts from Europe who had come to the United States as refugees in the 1930s joined American psychoanalysts in psychiatry departments as well as at independent institutes. They played a role during the 1950s and 1960s in moving American psychiatry from its traditional focus on custodial care in mental hospitals to an interest in psychotherapy, research into families of the mentally ill, and even the prevention of mental illness.

This was also the period of the initial growth of the National Institute of Mental Health (NIMH), which promulgated the idea that mental health and disease were grounded in social as well as biological conditions. It was assumed that families and parenting were, or could be, sources of mental illness, and during this period when much mental health research was focused directly or indirectly on parenting, the concept of parental influence enjoyed an important place—perhaps too important a place—in the public discourse connecting psychiatry with the social sciences. Other doctors—psychiatrists and psychoanalysts as well as psychologists—joined pediatricians as experts giving guidance to American parents. And in their best-selling books, they often blamed parents—usually mothers—for their children's mental illnesses, adjustment problems, and emotional disorders.

Thus, the mental health era of American parenting that was already under way when Benjamin Spock's book emancipated mothers from bondage to the pediatric expert provided fertile ground for increasing concern that mothers could jeopardize the emotional security of their children, possibly with damaging psychological effects. Later in the period, from the late 1970s onwards, other medical experts would point to psychological damage in cases of "battered" and sexually abused children, providing a new type of anxiety not only for parents but also for preschools and day care centers where young children were under the care of strangers. The words "trauma" and "abuse" were added to vernacular American speech as ordinary people came to assume that unpleasant or "adverse" events in childhood would have long-lasting deleterious effects on mental functioning.

There remained ambiguity about what was adverse and might have a long-term impact and what was not. The possibility was enough to make parents nervous, however, and it occasioned a deep change in parental style: toward making encouragement paramount and avoiding any hint of harshness in parental behavior because of the risk of emotional damage. There was an exchange of taboos: what had been forbidden (as recently as the 1930s) as "indulgence" was now necessary for mental health, and the formerly mandatory "discipline" was now seen as "abuse."

The best-known authors whose books blamed parents for mental disorders—Karen Horney, John Bowlby, and Bruno Bettelheim—were psychoanalysts, but their theories departed from Freud's. While Freud had emphasized childhood experience as a source of neurosis and deplored society's censorious attitude toward sexuality, he did not believe that children were blank slates. On the contrary, he claimed that the development of children was largely determined by phylogeny—that is, evolution—and

that universal "psychosexual" stages based on neurological maturation permitted only a narrow window through which parents
could exert a positive or negative influence on a child's psychological development.

During infancy, for example, a child was in the "oral" stage
in which her "intrapsychic experience," with the potential of
long-term psychological influence, was sensitive only to the pleasure or deprivation associated with being fed; the impact of the
mother was mediated through her role in the feeding experience,
not through those other social or communicative channels that
would later be known as "interpersonal." This model, including
the subsequent "anal" and "genital" stages—also conceived of
as specific bodily sensitivities dictating limits on parental influence—was set forth by Freud in 1905 and became part of the
Freudian canon without validation from further research.[17] It
was never repudiated by Freud or his followers, despite many
of Freud's own later formulations suggesting processes of social
influence on the child's psychological development (for example,
the "identification" of the boy with his father, resulting in an in-
ternalized "superego" or moral conscience).[18]

By the mid-1930s, leaders of Freud's circle in Vienna, like
Heinz Hartmann and Anna Freud, as well as Melanie Klein in
London, recognized in their writings that there was more to early
child experience than the psychosexual stages, but those close to
the master attempted to make such recognition compatible with
his oral-anal-genital framework. Others were ready to make an
open break from the original formulation, with its implications of
biological determinism and innate constraints on parental influence. And while Freud was not inclined to give advice to parents,
some of these renegade psychoanalysts were eager to do so.

The post-Freudian psychoanalysts who flourished in the United
States and to some extent in England reshaped the theory to fit

the environmentalism of popular and philosophical thought in those countries, giving far greater scope to parental influence than the Freudian theoretical model did. Karen Horney is a case in point. She had been a senior teacher at the Berlin Psychoanalytic Institute, but in America she became a leader of the "neo-Freudian" movement. (The other leaders were Erich Fromm and Harry Stack Sullivan.) Her best-selling books *The Neurotic Personality of Our Time* (1937) and *New Ways in Psychoanalysis* (1939) and other books published after the war, such as *Neurosis and Human Growth* (1950), claimed that all children have a need for emotional security that, when thwarted by distant, often self-absorbed parents, creates a "basic anxiety" that leads to neurosis.[19] "Like any other living organism, the human individual needs favorable conditions for his growth 'from acorn into oak tree'; he needs an atmosphere of warmth to give him both a feeling of security and the inner freedom to have his own feelings and thoughts and to express himself."[20] This was a far cry from Freudian theory, and Horney was forced out of the New York Psychoanalytic Institute, but her ideas seemed to fit the American mood at a time when *security* was a prevalent metaphor for what Americans had lacked in the 1930s (economic security) and what they had gained from Roosevelt's New Deal (Social Security). Parents of the previous generation, known to Horney through the recollections of her adult patients, were to be blamed for not meeting the emotional needs of their children and leaving them insecure and with a basic anxiety that formed neuroses requiring treatment in psychotherapy.

John Bowlby, a British psychoanalyst and initially a protégé of Freud's student Melanie Klein, was directly concerned with children in institutions and at home. In his 1953 book *Child Care and the Growth of Love,* which sold 450,000 copies in the English-language edition, Bowlby stated, "Mother-love is as important for mental health as are vitamins and proteins for physical health," directly contradicting Watson's views of twenty-five years earlier. He coined the term "maternal deprivation" and called for warmth, love, and proximity in infant and child care.[21] Bowlby's writings were aimed at reforming institutional care for children. Calling attention to research indicating the apparent damage to the psychological development of children raised in orphanages that provided no affectionate care, Bowlby helped bring about fundamental changes in public policies concerning the treatment of children without parents. His attempts to apply his findings to home-reared children and specify the amount of time that mothers *caring for their own infants* should leave them with others, however, proved far more controversial and led to criticisms of his concept of "maternal deprivation."[22]

In retrospect, Bowlby took his vitamin metaphor too literally. Likening the affect-starvation of children in orphanages to a nutritional disease in which a single nutrient like vitamin C was absent, Bowlby assumed that the amount of mother-love needed to prevent mental and moral disorders in family-reared children could be readily assessed and prescribed. But this was problematic, and subsequent efforts to demonstrate a cause-effect relationship between "maternal sensitivity to infant signals" and "secure attachment" led to a gross exaggeration of the potential for mental disorders in the general population of mothers and infants.[23]

For Bowlby and Mary Ainsworth, as with Horney, "security" was the key factor in mentally healthy development; thus, children "insecurely attached" to their mothers were at risk. Horney and Bowlby empathized with a generation who resented the "distant" parental care they had received in the 1920s and 1930s, when hygiene and discipline were the orders of the day. In that sense they could be seen as advocates for that generation, the victims of "bad" parenting. Revenge was found in formulating the charge against their parents as putting their children at risk for psychopathology. But Horney and Bowlby were also warning parents in the 1950s that their own caregiving behavior could put their children at risk for serious mental illness. The stakes involved in parenting had been raised.

In this era, the 1950s and 1960s, the neo-Freudian analysts and other academic and medical experts went beyond Horney's blaming of mothers for their children's neuroses to hold them responsible for more serious mental disorders, including schizophrenia and autism. Harry Stack Sullivan formulated an account of schizophrenia as based on the child's earliest interactions with his parents.[24] His colleague Frieda Fromm-Reichmann, a psychoanalyst, coined the term "schizophrenogenic mother" to identify the mother—her behavior and personality—as the cause of the schizophrenic's mental illness in adulthood.[25] In 1956 the anthropologist Gregory Bateson, the psychiatrist John Weakland, and the family therapist Jay Haley[26] proposed the "double-bind hypothesis" that emotionally inconsistent mothering could explain how schizophrenogenic mothers operated. But as Bateson's biographer tells us, Bateson formulated the hypothesis without any data; indeed, he "pulled [it] out of the sky, on the basis of looking at the way people communicated."[27] These ideas were nonetheless very influential at the time, at least until the 1970s.

Later scholars would look back at this period and the widespread acceptance of the schizophrenogenic mother almost with disbelief. The Harvard historian of science Anne Harrington, in a 2012 article, "The Fall of the Schizophrenogenic Mother," published in *The Lancet,* states: "Today, memories of that whole era make many people wince. Schizophrenia is now understood to be a brain disorder, best treated with medication. The psychiatric profession is appalled by the burden and pain that was once inflicted by telling families, and especially mothers, that they had literally driven their children crazy."[28] Yet, as Harrington points out, neurobiological research was not the only reason for the change between then and now. There was also the feminist movement, the deinstitutionalization of mental hospitals, which sent so many schizophrenics home, the claims of radical therapists like R. D. Laing that no one is normal, and—most poignantly—the formation by family caregivers of a movement called the National Alliance on Mental Illness.[29] A spokesman for that organization declared before the World Congress on Psychiatry in 1977, "We failed to understand why parents of a child with leukemia were treated with sympathy and understanding, while parents of a child with schizophrenia were treated with scorn and condemnation."[30] Finally, and most ironically, in 1983 Thomas McGlashan, one of Fromm-Reichmann's successors in the psychoanalytic treatment of schizophrenics at Chestnut Lodge, a psychiatric hospital in Maryland, publicly presented his analysis of the case records of 446 patients on the effectiveness of the treatment: "The data are in. The experiment failed."[31]

Mothers were also blamed for autism during this period. Leo Kanner of Johns Hopkins Medical School claimed that "infantile autism," as he named it, was caused by "refrigerator mothers" who were lacking in warmth, but he later abandoned that hypothesis. However, Bruno Bettelheim, in *The Empty Fortress,* formulated the more extreme idea that "the precipitating factor in infantile autism is the parent's wish that his child should not exist."[32]

These unproven theories, though controversial even when formulated, were widely disseminated and influential in psychiatric as well as public discussions of mental disease, and they added to the burden of guilt carried by many mothers of schizophrenic and autistic children. The theories were not supported by later research and are no longer taken seriously, but the terror they spread among mothers—that their care might permanently damage their children—had long-term effects on generations of mothers. Bettelheim's best-selling books, beginning with his first book, *Love Is Not Enough* (1950), were particularly ferocious about the foibles of parents.[33] During his years as our colleague at the University of Chicago, Bettelheim emerged as the doyen of the parent-blamers, and he liked to confront mothers with what he regarded as their sins. At one time we were friendly with him and his wife, and Sarah made the mistake of mentioning that we were having trouble toilet training our two-year-old daughter Anna. Bruno immediately seized upon the fact that Sarah usually wore a brown sweater and related its (supposedly fecal) color to Anna's difficulties. This reaction was typical of Bettelheim's approach and its effects: he shot from the hip with an immediate explanation, was always certain the mother was to blame, and invoked his authority as a clinician to overcome opposition to his far-fetched explanation. In fact, he often got mothers to accept blame, and the popularity of his books suggests that more than a few Americans at the time found his claims plausible.

At the very beginning of *Love Is Not Enough*, which introduced the public to the Orthogenic School, his residential treatment center for disturbed children, Bettelheim tells the reader: "All the children who live there are free of physical disorder, but suffer from severe emotional disturbances that have proved (or are expected to prove) beyond the reach of the common therapeutic techniques. . . . The difficulties of almost all emotionally disturbed children have originated in the relationship to a parent."[34] This raises the question of what it is parents do or fail to do that causes such severe disorders, and Bettelheim's answer is, in effect, that their overtly loving acts, such as cuddling, and expressions of approval are empty gestures unaccompanied by the genuine feelings from which the child can gain a sense of comfort and protection. In contrast with Horney's affectionless parents or Bowlby's observably sterile institutions, the Orthogenic School's parents are portrayed as having been affectionate to a child who nevertheless ended up with a severe disturbance because the parents' emotions *were not genuine*. So what Bettelheim meant by the title of the book was that loving *acts* are not enough; they must be accompanied by sincere emotions or the child will become emotionally disturbed. "Thus it is not even enough to do the right thing at the right moment, it must also be done with emotions that belong to the act."[35]

Bettelheim saves his greatest censure for the hypocrisy of parents whose feelings do not match their actions, who satisfy their own need *to look like* good modern parents while not considering what the child really needs. This enables him to assume the role of a rebel against modern trends while raising the bar for considerate mothering even higher. He says that a child who wets his bed, for example, "needs" to be chastised; when a mother decides to excuse the infraction, she is supporting her self-image as a kind, modern parent at the expense of the child's appropriate training. Does this kind of mistake lead to severe emotional disturbance? Yes, says Bettelheim, presenting an outré clinical conjecture as if it were a proven fact and applying it to the full range of children in the School, which included those diagnosed as schizophrenic. If this seems outrageous now, it was nonetheless enough to worry many mothers in 1950.

The peak of parent-blaming (or mother-bashing) in Bettelheim's career came with his claim that maternal attitudes caused autism. *The Empty Fortress* was published just as empirical research was beginning to suggest organic causes for autism, but public (and even expert) opinion in 1967 accepted parental influence as equally or more credible, and Bruno Bettelheim was a famous authority. He won the media battle, with rave reviews for his best-selling book, but (eventually) lost the scientific war. For many years, however, parents of autistic children stood blamed for their sins in causing their children's disorders.

The messages for parents in these popular books and other mental health literature of the time were disseminated through women's magazines, which were widely read by mothers during the postwar period. Spock had a regular column in *McCall's*, and Bettelheim wrote for the *Ladies' Home Journal*. Other magazines— *Redbook, Woman's Home Companion, Good Housekeeping, Parents* magazine—brought mothers the latest trends in parenting, often taken directly from the books just mentioned. In addition, the newsmagazines *Time* and *Newsweek* published articles on parental influence. The mass media's "pop psychology" was always buttressed with advice from certified experts on mental health and with selected evidence from empirical research.

These ideas about the dangers that parenting presents to the mental health of children are no longer new, nor are they considered credible by most psychiatrists and child psychologists nowadays, but they cast a long shadow onto current parenting practices in the English-speaking world—especially in the avoidance of harshness with young children—and onto psychological theories about parents' influence on child development.

Questioning Attachment Theory: A Global Perspective

The longest shadow from theories of the 1960s cast on current conceptions of parental influence has been that of the Bowlby-Ainsworth model of infant attachment, with its prediction that babies whose mothers were "insensitive" to their signals during the first year (largely between six and twelve months) would

be "insecurely attached" at one year of age and grow up emotionally disturbed thereafter. A national study organized by the
US National Institute of Child Health and Human Development (NICHD) showed in 1997 that 38 percent of one-year-olds
were classified as insecurely attached, suggesting something
close to an epidemic of emotional disturbance in the American
population—if you believed the Bowlby-Ainsworth model.[36] But
there are reasons to doubt its validity, particularly if you take seriously the evidence from other cultures.

The Bowlby-Ainsworth model presupposes that each baby
who becomes *securely* attached by twelve months of age has a
mother who has been sensitive to his signals and who continues
to be responsible for his care as he grows up. Without infant care
that fosters secure attachment in this way, the infant is said to be
at risk for mental disturbance. As we will see in later chapters,
however, there are parts of the world in which these assumptions
do not hold:

- Among various African populations (the Hausa, Efe, Beng)
  mothers hold and breast-feed each other's infants and comfort them in other ways so that the babies may become
  attached to several women living in the same household
  or nearby households. What are the implications for the
  future mental health of these babies? Is their attachment
  security greater than that of Western infants because they
  receive more attentive care in the aggregate, less because
  care is distributed among more caregivers, or the same because of some unidentified ceiling effect on security for all
  humans? There is no evidence to answer these questions,
  but it seems clear that there are more pathways to subjec-
  tive security—and probably more types of "security"—than
  Bowlby and Ainsworth imagined.

- One potential pathway to the child's emotional security, widely found in Africa and elsewhere (and described in Chapter 4), is through skin-to-skin infant care, with tactile mother-infant contact day and night, co-sleeping, responsive breast-feeding, and keeping infants as calm as possible at all times. The only predictor of emotional security measured in the Bowlby-Ainsworth system is "sensitivity to infant signals," which gives a privileged place to the infant's cry heard by the mother across a distance as the trigger of care. This excludes the continuous tactile experience, which may prevent the infant's need to cry, as a factor.

- In West Africa and many of the Pacific Islands, toddlers are sent away by their mothers after weaning and taken care of by their grandmothers or other women. In some societies, like the Mende of Sierra Leone, a majority of children have this experience. If young children's separation from their mothers early in life is as injurious psychologically as Bowlby postulated, this should lead to widespread emotional disturbance in these populations. Once again, there have been no developmental studies to address this possibility, but until we have reports of widespread emotional disturbance in these societies due to early separation, rather than assume the theory is right, we question the prediction and its theory based in our culture.

- Some mothers, like those we observed among the Gusii of Kenya, care for their own children and are consistently responsive to their infants' cries of distress but, unlike Westerners, are consistently *un*responsive to their babbles. Thus, it is unclear whether these mothers should be considered "highly sensitive" (by their cultural standards), "highly insensitive" (by ours), or intermediate (if responses are averaged across infant signals). This kind of problem was not anticipated by the Bowlby-Ainsworth conceptualization, which is focused more on evaluating maternal behavior than on understanding its complexity.

These are some of the problems left unsolved by attachment psychology in its failure to examine whether its model of secure attachment—based as much in a twentieth-century Anglo-American moral ideology as it is in developmental research—holds elsewhere in the world. The Bowlby-Ainsworth model's claim that the mental health of 38 percent of American children has been jeopardized by insensitive mothering during infancy might well predict even higher frequencies of disturbed development for children raised under the conditions prevalent in other cultures.

As increasing numbers of American mothers joined the workforce between 1970 and 1990, infants were more frequently cared for by others. Bowlby, ever the advocate of maternal care, told an interviewer in 1974: "Day-care is a dangerous waste of time and money."[37] But when the NICHD carried out that large study, no greater frequency of insecure attachment was found among infants in day care.[38] That remains the last word on the subject, suggesting once again that the pathological outcomes claimed by attachment theorists do not stand up to careful examination.

The inadequacy of attachment theory, after forty-five years and thousands of apparently scientific studies that convince fewer and fewer researchers, raises questions about the credibility of its forecasts of parental influence. As we read the evidence, attachment theory's lack of attention to cultural variation in the contexts and patterns of infant care—leaving out how most human infants are being (or have been) raised—has left the Bowlby-Ainsworth model fatally flawed.[39] Moreover, is it credible that a single behavior measured at twelve months of age determines the course of later psychological development? Should parents believe that it's all over after the first year—or, for that matter, that psychological health or child development in general can be reduced to emotional security?

Unfortunately, the sorry state of attachment theory is symptomatic of problems with past and present theories of parental influence, which have also tended to make inflated claims of lifelong psychological impact and universality in the human species and to hold parents responsible for the mental, moral, and educational problems of their children. Parental practices, as we shall see in this book, vary much too widely across cultures for us to accept uncritically the supposition that the mental health of American children is being put at risk by "insensitive" infant care.

Experts Versus Parents

In this overview of expert-guided parenting in America since the late nineteenth century, we have seen how experts—in public health, pediatrics, and psychiatry—provided advice that claimed the authority of science while blending moral ideology with (incomplete) empirical evidence. In retrospect, much of this expert advice was unscientific despite its empirical content. Yet we have also argued that some ideas about parenting have proved wrong, implying that our knowledge has grown in a way we associate with science. We have not given up on the notion that parenting can be informed by science, and in our time we look to child development research, especially developmental psychology, for scientific knowledge. But when it comes to parental influence, we may be expecting too much. Jerome Kagan, a child psychologist who has devoted his long life to the rigorous study of development from infancy to adulthood, has this to say:

Why, then, do many psychologists, psychiatrists, and parents continue to believe in a strong connection between the experiences of early childhood and the young adult's psychological profile? The immaturity of our understanding of development, which rests on weak theory, insensitive methods, and the absence of a tapestry of firm facts, is one reason. This unfortunate state of affairs allows the scientists who believe in connectivity to maintain their faith in a strong predictive relation between early childhood and adulthood. No contemporary fact requires the committed advocates of infant determinism to relinquish their favorite premise.

The possibility that the representations of the emotional experiences of the first two years no longer exert any influence on adolescents is as reasonable as the assumption that they do.

The evidence gathered over the past thirty years, albeit inconclusive, has shifted the burden of proof from those who had been skeptical of strong preservation to those who believe in the indefinite preservation of the products of early experiences. That is progress![40]

Kagan's case for the inconclusiveness of research on parental influence is based partly on the multiplicity of factors (including innate temperament and brain maturation) that can influence psychological outcomes and partly on the context-sensitive nature of childhood experience and parental practices—the latter referring to the variable social and cultural environments in which children grow up. He takes his colleagues in psychology to task for using methods of dubious validity (for example, questionnaires and interviews when observations are called for) and for their relentless focus on testing available hypotheses rather than engaging in unfettered exploration. Thus, one of the leading figures in child psychology casts doubt on our current knowledge of parental influence.

Does this mean we should give up looking to psychology for answers to questions about parental influence? Not necessarily. There are some psychologists and anthropologists (not enough) who have specialized in the comparative study of parenting and child development, and in the next chapters we turn to their work for new light on parental influence.

∾ 2 ∾

Expecting: Pregnancy and Birth

WHEN SARAH TOLD expectant mothers in our Kenyan infant study that some American women say they never feel so good as when they're pregnant—at least after the first trimester— and that we have an expression, "the bloom of pregnancy," the Gusii women couldn't believe it. They claimed to detest pregnancy, pointing especially to the nausea and vomiting of what we call morning sickness, which for many Gusii mothers is not restricted to the first trimester but continues throughout pregnancy, and to the difficulty of working in the fields when pregnant. Yet these were women who gave birth ten times on average. We came to believe that, whatever the actual complications of pregnancy, they exaggerated their aversion to the process because they feared that—following the Gusii witchcraft narrative—were they to reveal, even to an outsider like Sarah, how much they *wanted* to bear children, it would elicit the ill will of other women. What they really wanted, but could not bring themselves to affirm, was to bear a child every two years until menopause, not only to keep up with other women in the family and neighborhood but also to reassure themselves that their reproductive capacity had not already been impaired by the ill will (witchcraft) of others—another concern they could not allow themselves to talk about.

Gusii mothers also told Sarah that, unlike American women, they never announced to any of the women around them (their mothers-in-law, sisters-in-law, co-wives, and neighbors), "I'm pregnant!" Why? Because "they will find out when they hear me vomiting in the morning and later when they see my stomach." Sarah offered our own logic—since others were bound to find out, why not tell them? The women answered, "Since they will certainly find out, I don't *need* to tell them." The act of (deliberately) revealing one's pregnancy would be understood as flaunting an advantage over others, and such flaunting would elicit jealousy and lead to witchcraft. When Sarah asked, "What about confiding in a woman who has many living children and grandchildren herself?" they said, "It doesn't matter—someone else might overhear." The act of announcing the good news of one's pregnancy would automatically endanger the self and had to be avoided. In the Gusii context, then, women felt too vulnerable to the potential of witchcraft to discuss their pregnancy experiences with other women.[1]

According to Gusii tradition, a woman gives birth at home (her mother's for the first child, her husband's thereafter) with older women of the neighborhood in attendance. If the labor is lengthy by their standards, they shout at her to confess to adultery and might slap and pinch her as well. A midwife, called only for a difficult birth, might give her an herbal formula to facilitate the delivery; as we discovered, it also retarded expulsion of the placenta. We took several women to the hospital with retained placentas. At the time, however, few had hospital deliveries.

A woman who had a poor relationship with her husband's family might find herself giving birth alone or with inadequate help. Given her fear of jealousy and witchcraft, she might even elect to give birth alone. Mary, the most educated woman of our sample mothers (ten years of schooling), reported that when she went into labor (at age eighteen) with her first child, she chose to give birth by herself in the fields. Another young woman, named Trufena, went into labor with her second child while Sarah was interviewing her. Like Mary, Trufena had been to high school. As a student, she had eloped with her sweetheart, who came from a less affluent family than she did. And therein lay the problem: her in-laws, seeing her as arrogant and disrespectful, disliked her. When she admitted to Sarah and her assistant that she was in labor (no doubt she'd been having contractions for some time but, being in most respects a traditional Gusii woman, had made no sign), they sent for a midwife from a neighboring community and for Trufena's mother-in-law, who arrived somewhat inebriated from a nearby beer-drink with a group of women friends.[2] Instead of coming into the kitchen where Trufena was pacing, they stayed in the living room. Thus it was that Sarah and her assistant found themselves delivering the baby. The midwife, a woman in her sixties, arrived after Trufena's infant son had been born.

Rituals of Pregnancy and Birth

Humans, unlike other mammals and primates, complicate our reproductive processes with cultural symbols that can evoke diametrically opposite feelings: Is pregnancy a blessing or a curse? Does it bring purity or pollution, vulnerability or strength? The answers, and the practices that embody them, vary across cultures, even in our contemporary world.

Before the spread of scientific medicine, with its clinics, hospitals, and public health programs, pregnancy and birth were understood and dealt with in terms of traditional concepts and

practices—including ones we would characterize as supernatural, religious, or spiritual. In much of the world these practices
and concepts have survived alongside bureaucratically organized
modern medicine. In other words, the meanings of human reproduction remain variable in emotional as well as intellectual terms
and in terms of the social practices that express them.

When Sarah was pregnant with our first child, Bob accompanied her to Lamaze "natural childbirth" lessons, where she
learned to "pant and blow" during delivery and he to give her
support. But when she gave birth to Anna in a Chicago hospital,
Bob was excluded from the delivery room, like all other fathers
(according to the laws of Cook County, Illinois), and joined the
others smoking in the waiting room as they waited for news of
their children's birth. Three years later, when Sarah gave birth to
our second child in the same hospital, the law had changed and
Bob was able to be with Sarah in the delivery room when Alex
was born. In that short period of time, Bob's experience at birth
had changed from that of, for example, fathers in Africa, who
are absent when their wives deliver, to that of fathers among the
Yucatec Maya, who are present as assistants at their children's
births. But the presence or absence of fathers is just one aspect
of cultural variation in birth practices.

South Asia

Among the Hindu and Buddhist peoples of India, Sri Lanka,
and Nepal, there is great concern about purity and pollution,
and women's bodies are prime sources of pollution, especially
from menstruation and birth. Women are also in charge of
the rituals that maintain purity in the home. During the first
months of pregnancy, however, a practice in Sri Lanka and parts
of India called *dola-duka* puts women in an unusually privileged
position, though only temporarily: they experience cravings

for particular, even exotic, foods, and their usually dominant husbands must provide these foods, whatever the difficulty or expense. Meanwhile, the pregnant wife suspends her regular work routine and relaxes at home. This status reversal is man-datory—to ignore the wife's cravings would be sinful. By the time she reaches the fifth month of pregnancy, however, the exceptional period is over.[3]

In the north Indian village of "Shanti Nagar" in Haryana state, studied by the anthropologists Ruth and Stanley Freed in 1958–1959:

Public announcements of conception did not occur. The hus-band of a young bride was usually advised of her pregnancy by his mother or a senior woman in the house or through circumlo-cution by his wife. The mother-in-law, who usually was the first to know even before the pregnant bride, spread the word so that shortly all the women in the lineage and caste knew and so did the neighbors. . . . Who was pregnant, for how long, and when the child was expected, were facts known by all women. For example, in one brief conversation an informant revealed that an older Brahman's wife was one to two months pregnant, that she had had four children who had died and one living son, that a Jat (farming caste) woman, who so far had borne four girls, would have her child in two months, and that another Brahman woman was expecting her fourth child. . . .

Discussions of pregnancies and sexual relations differed with males. Although they discussed births and birth ceremonies with us when asked, they were not interested in the details . . . and so they were not well informed about them. . . . Except for conception, they had little or nothing to do with birth, prena-tal care, delivery or child rearing practices for infants and small children. . . .

Even in fairly well-off families in Shanti Nagar, the women continued to work both in the fields and household almost until the time of delivery. During the last month of pregnancy there was some reduction in work.[4]

After giving birth, the woman is in a state of pollution. Here is an account of birth pollution from the Tibetan Buddhist Zangskar people of Ladakh in the Himalayan region of India:

> Childbirth transforms both the mother and her newborn into social outcastes, who are confined in order to avoid polluting the village space. The postbirth seclusion . . . can last between a week and a month, depending on the village deity. The mother must stay inside the house and stoop when passing a window that faces the village altar or temple. Inside the house, she must avoid the hearth and eats from a separate cup and plate. In extreme cases, she may be a virtual prisoner in her room, where she is passed food and drink through the door. The husband or a male affine [in-law] who cuts the umbilical cord is the only other person who may face some ritual seclusion. . . . The house itself becomes polluted during the seclusion period, and other villagers—except clan members—avoid eating there. One week after the birth, the household itself can reopen its doors and resume reciprocal relations. It will invite a monk to perform a purification rite.[5]

Zangskar women are prohibited from delivering a child in their own parents' home rather than their husband's home, where they live. One woman who broke the rule suffered twelve hours of "excruciating back pain" during labor; she "blamed her natal deity, the four-armed Mahakala . . . , who was considered especially strict regarding pollution practices."[6]

There are variations across South Asia in the details of birth pollution. Among the rural Hindus (Brahmin-Chetri) of Nepal, the mother but not the child is polluted, and the period of pollution begins with the cutting of the umbilical cord and extends until the eleventh day after birth. It is only after an astrologer has been consulted to ascertain that the child was not born under a sign hostile to the father that the father is allowed to see his child.[7]

These brief glimpses of South Asian rituals of pregnancy and childbirth indicate how deeply cultural symbols permeate a mother's experience, in the context of a sacred scriptural tradition, and with highly specific rules sometimes enforced by clerical authority. As in our African observations, there are negative emotions, especially fear, in some of these experiences. We might see fear as realistic, given the considerable risks of death for both mother and child in these settings. But the cultural narratives and their symbols—involving concepts of witchcraft, female pollution, or angry deities—arouse *additional* fears, not of realistic survival risks from a biomedical viewpoint but of persons and spirits threatening mother and child. Ritual formulas intended to protect them may provide emotional comfort.

Midwives in Charge: Mexico and Central America

The indigenous peoples of Mexico and Central America have professional midwives who guide women's experience of pregnancy and childbirth. Among the Mayans of Guatemala, the midwife is sanctified in the indigenous religion and is identified at birth by special signs indicating her destiny to take on this role.[8] An expectant mother seeks her out by the fifth month of pregnancy, and the midwife massages her and gives her firm instructions concerning her conduct. The pregnant woman's food cravings are said to issue from the baby within and must be satisfied to avoid dire consequences. Other instructions are also intended to safeguard the fetus and mother from spiritual as well as natural dangers. At birth, the midwife is in charge, and one of her skills is inverting the fetus to avoid breech delivery. The husband and other men in the family are in attendance (in contrast with South Asia), and the husband may hold the woman from behind, as was the practice in Yucatán, but this may not be necessary if the woman is on the floor rather than in a hammock. Some midwives nowadays have had training in modern medicine, and there is a trend to replace the sacred midwives with medical practitioners and hospital deliveries. The Mayan example suggests that having a professional midwife (sacred or not) attending birth and guiding pregnancy is better for mothers than the dependence on female kin that prevails (or did until recently) in many parts of the agrarian world.

By the 1980s women in urban Mexico, as in much of the developing world, were increasingly likely to give birth in modern medical facilities (where, as some Cuernavaca mothers complained to Sarah, overburdened doctors, rather than wait out a lengthy natural delivery, too often performed caesarean sections). In rural areas, however, Sarah was often told that harried, uncaring (and mostly male) doctors were to be avoided. Thus, for educated and illiterate women alike, midwives remained the birth attendant of choice. Poorer women living on the outskirts of Tilzapotla, Morelos (where we worked from 1987 to 1991) were attended by traditional midwives who might or might not have taken a government midwifery course. Meanwhile, when a better-off woman "neared her time" (depending on how much help she could muster at home, this could be a week before her due date), she moved in with one of the town's two certified midwives, nurses who had additional midwifery training, to deliver her baby in a spacious "nursing home." Only if problems arose during delivery would she be transferred to the nearest hospital for delivery by a doctor—almost always by a dreaded caesarean.

Breech Births

There are many social and cultural variations in reproduction across human populations and historical periods. Take breech presentation—a child being born feet- or buttocks-first rather than headfirst—which occurs, though rarely (3 to 4 percent), in all populations. It can hardly be ignored, as the baby is often unusually small and both mother and baby are considered vulnerable to risks from such a birth. The question is, what do different peoples make of it, and do about it, and what are we to make of the variations? Here are three cases from differing cultures:

- *Botswana:* The !Kung San ("Bushmen") of the Kalahari Desert in Botswana are the classic example of African hunter-gatherers, and their reproductive practices have been carefully studied.[9] !Kung women give birth on average every four years, carrying the youngest one in a sling during the birth interval. They have a cultural ideal of unassisted birth. When a pregnant woman is near term and feels contractions, she goes off into the bush, quietly and often alone, to give birth. If there is a breech delivery, she buries the baby and returns to the village. A !Kung San man told the anthropologist Melvin Konner that if a baby born by breech presentation were kept, "people would talk about it and say it had no sense because it was born backwards."[10] Other birth anomalies are disposed of the same way.

- *Kenya:* When a Gusii woman gives birth by breech delivery (or has twins, an albino, or simply a small preterm infant), it is regarded as an omen that the husband's ancestors are distressed and will visit further reproductive disasters on the mother—meaning infertility or dead and disabled children—unless an elaborate ritual is performed. A local midwife (called only for difficult deliveries) and older women in the family decide that mother and baby must go into a ritual seclusion (in her own house) for protection; the rituals are overseen by a woman who has had the same birth anomaly (in this case breech presentation) and has had additional training that certifies her as an *omokorerani* (practitioner). We observed the rituals specified by such practitioners for one breech birth and two twin births in a Gusii community. Mother and newborn were considered to be highly vulnerable to the potential malevolence of neighbors, and they were kept at home next to the placenta, which was placed in a bowl and covered by leaves, with the cooking fire kept going day and night.[11] The idea is to keep them especially warm, with the placenta symbolically lending protection from harm. The placenta is not buried until the husband arrives, often from a distance if he is working outside the district, and after its burial no one can visit mother and child who did not do so during the period of placental protection. With none of her usual tasks to perform, the mother holds the baby in her arms and on her body, permitting frequent breast-feeding. These practices (that is, constant mother-infant contact, frequent breast-feeding, special warmth) are basically identical to the "kangaroo maternal care" recommended by UNICEF for small preterm babies, and many breech babies and twins actually are small, preterm, and fragile. Once the husband has consulted a diviner and purchased a goat of the right color for sacrifice by a male elder of the lineage, a ritual of emergence is performed and mother and baby are presented to their kin and other neighbors. The ancestors have been placated, the baby and mother have recovered, and they are ritually protected from the ill will of their neighbors.

- *Central America:* The Mayans of Central America are an agrarian people with a history of centralized political systems and many specialized roles, including midwife. Being a midwife was a sacred calling, identified at a woman's birth, and Mayan midwives were noted for their skills in managing pregnancy (from five months onwards) and delivery. One such skill was monitoring the position of the fetus, and another was the "external cephalic version" of the fetus—that is, massaging the mother's abdomen so as to turn the baby from a breech presentation to a headfirst position, in advance of delivery. This practice was recorded by Spanish missionaries among not only the Mayans but other Mesoamerican peoples in documents dating as far back as 1547, as well as by twentieth-century social scientists, who took photographs.[12] Rather than react after the fact, the Mayan midwife *prevented* breech births.

One interpretation of these remarkably varied ways of reacting to and managing breech birth would be that they represent *progress*—from a "primitive" past of hunter-gatherers unable to deal with the problem except by disposing of the newborn; to the more "advanced" level of African agriculturalists, whose practices provide bodily protection for the vulnerable child after birth in an elaborate ritual; and culminating in the "most advanced" level of the

Mayans, endowed with a specialized skill that *prevents* the obstetrical problem, using a technique bordering on modern medicine.

This progressive narrative seems at first to fit the three-culture comparison, but it is erroneous in the light of more evidence. To begin with, the narrative tends to disregard the potential adaptive values of each set of practices when examined in its local context. Among the !Kung San, selective infanticide, it has been argued, is adaptive: the lengthy (four-year) birth interval, in permitting a woman to be mobile enough for food-gathering, requires her to select which of her offspring are to survive. A woman who has twins does not keep both babies because two would encumber her, so one must be buried; a baby with an apparent birth defect would seem to be too unlikely to survive to warrant a mother's energy investment. Furthermore, infanticide is not limited to societies at the hunting-gathering level of technology and socioeconomic development: agrarian societies in India, China, and eighteenth-century Europe practiced it, and it still occurs in South Asia.[13]

Second, these differences in management of breech births do not represent a progression from irrational symbol systems to rational thought. All three responses to breech presentation are embedded in ideas or symbol systems that can hardly be called rational. The Mayan midwife, for example, destined to play that role by the conditions of her own birth, is said to be imperiled by supernatural disasters should she choose to refuse her calling. Her lengthy practice as a birth attendant leads her to understand through experience how to turn the fetus headfirst through massage, but this is not based on biomedical science. She is both a spiritual and empirical practitioner.

The Question of Progress: America and China

Societies with modern medicine do not always retain their advantage. In the United States, midwives were largely driven out of business in the early twentieth century with the professionalization of medicine, and the midwives' practice of turning the fetus to prevent a breech birth (as their Mayan counterparts did) was replaced by caesarean section, a surgical procedure carrying greater risks. This is not progress, as recognized by the World Health Organization (WHO) and other medical bodies that have deplored the high frequency of caesareans in the United States: almost one-third of births, more than double the WHO-recommended frequency of 10 to 15 percent.

The Mayans (and other indigenous Mesoamericans) were not alone in devising premodern solutions to the problem of breech births. In Chinese traditional medicine, moxibustion is a method that uses the heat generated by burning herbal preparations containing *Artemisia vulgaris* (mugwort) to stimulate acupuncture points. The application of moxibustion to acupoint BL67 (*Zhiyin*), located beside the outer corner of the fifth toenail—that is, the nail of the little toe—of a mother with a fetus in the breech position is said to stimulate the fetus to move into the vertex, or headfirst, position.

What validity does this practice have in empirical terms? Drs. Francesco Cardini and Huang Weixin conducted a randomized controlled trial of 260 new mothers with breech fetuses in the thirty-third week of gestation in Nanchang, China, and published the results in the *Journal of the American Medical Association*.[14] They found that 75 percent of those in the moxibustion group gave birth to headfirst babies, whereas only 48 percent of those in the control group did; this is a highly significant difference, especially given the fact that a fetus tends naturally to move from the breech to the vertex position. Here again, an ancient birth practice seems to prevent breech delivery with minimal risk—the type of solution normally unavailable to women giving birth in a strictly modern American medical context.

Are we to conclude from these comparisons that there is no progress in science? On the contrary, it seems more likely that progress, in the sense of continued improvement, is an attribute of science that can be wrongly generalized to other aspects of culture. The breech position of a fetus as a biological fact—its place in the reproductive process and the risks associated with its lasting until birth—is far better understood by science than it was a century ago. The actual management of a breech delivery, however, is based on symbolic meanings in particular cultures and the demands of their socioeconomic institutions. As birth has been "medicalized"—institutionalized by Western standards in hospitals, clinics, and public health programs that have spread to most parts of the world during the last century—it may appear at first that reproduction has been rationalized once and for all in scientific terms. The casting aside of midwives' practical knowledge and the overuse of caesarean deliveries suggest otherwise. Medicalized or not, parents' experience of pregnancy and birth reflects local conceptions of how the lives of men or women are to be lived.

∾ 3 ∾

Infant Care: A World of Questions . . .
and Some Answers

PARENTS IN AMERICA and Britain, as we saw in Chapter 1, have been heavily influenced by experts—doctors and psychologists—based on research or clinical experience claimed to be scientific. But some claims are more credible than others. When a prominent psychiatrist states that "mother-love" is as necessary for a baby's healthy development as vitamin D, a mother has to decide whether to take this assertion literally or dismiss it as hyperbole.[1] Nutritional science shows how vitamin D intake from diet and sun exposure contributes to child health, and what happens when children are deprived of vitamin D (the crippling disease called rickets). But scientific knowledge concerning the influence of "mother-love" on infant development is hardly so well established, nor is it easily disentangled from moral judgments about good and bad mothering. Psychiatric and psychological experts often provide advice to American parents grounded in familiar assumptions about our standards of maternal care for infants. Their advice about what babies need for their healthy *emotional* development does not match in credibility that of experts on the dietary nutrients necessary for the healthy development of infants' bodies.

Infants: Risks in the First Year

Infancy has its risks, real and imagined. The most obvious risks, as assessed by biomedical science, are largely infectious diseases, which once killed 20 percent or more of infants during their first twelve months but diminished greatly in the last century, when infant mortality was reduced to only 5 percent on average in the developing (agrarian) world and to a far lower level—*half of 1 percent*—in our own and other developed countries. Thus, there remains a great divide: infants in the poorer, predominantly agrarian countries die ten times more frequently than infants in modern urban-industrial societies today; in India and its neighbors, the rate is about twelve times higher than in the most developed countries, and in sub-Saharan Africa almost twenty times higher.[2] The United Nations, in its Millennium Development Goals, aims to close the gap through concerted maternal and child health programs.[3]

It is important to consider health risks in infancy, but it could be misleading if American parents were to assume that the unfamiliar, and poorly understood, infant care practices of other countries are necessarily riskier than our own. Even more misleading is the assumption that the social and psychological environment of the baby is as measurable by a universal standard (usually formulated by a Western psychologist) as the risk of infection. The danger—and likelihood—is that Americans will apply standards of maternal care derived from their own current practices to other cultural contexts, on the assumption that the mothering practices of the poorer countries with high infant mortality rates *must* be putting babies at risk psychologically as well as medically—or that mothers in those countries necessarily decide that it is not worth struggling for the lives of their endangered babies.

The first question here is whether or not to see the greater risks to children in moral terms. Yes, the nineteenth-century Western movements to improve the conditions for other people's children were moral campaigns. It is furthermore true that a critical element in the great divide is that the Western countries adopted water purification, sewage disposal, garbage collection, and pasteurization of milk for *all* of their citizens more than a century ago, while in many developing countries these public health measures are still unavailable to the unprivileged majority. Extending the moral argument, the "child survival revolution" that brought down mortality rates in the later twentieth century was driven in part by the moral crusade of James Grant, director of UNICEF from 1980 to 1995, who relentlessly shamed the United Nations and powerful countries into making the saving of the lives of children in developing countries a high priority.[4]

Does that mean we Westerners care more about children in developing countries than their own parents do? No, this cannot be accepted as an explanation of the child survival revolution when we know the explicit moral doctrines that have motivated the commitment to save children without knowing the morality of the mothers in similar depth. Historians used to assume that in the past, when child death rates were high, infant death was a routine event to European mothers and they did not mourn. This was not true of the mothers we have observed in societies with high mortality rates; thus, we are skeptical of reports that attribute such responses to an entire population of mothers. Knowing how prone Westerners are to viewing death in moral terms, we withhold judgment until we can evaluate the data pro and con.

This is not to deny the evidence for infanticide, the abandonment of babies, and the selective neglect of female children as established and tolerated practices at many times and places. But it is to assert that Americans and other Westerners rush to moral judgments of abuse and neglect before gaining knowledge sufficient to comprehend how the parenting practices of diverse peoples should be interpreted.

We know, for example, that the use of swaddling and cradleboards in infant care is limited to peoples who live under conditions where freezing temperatures are regularly experienced.[5] That seems adaptive, but do these devices retard development or interfere with the mother-child relationship? Close studies among the Hopi and Navajo of the US Southwest indicate that cradleboards do not retard motor development and that observable differences between babies on cradleboards and those raised without them are "transient."[6] There is no evidence to support the notion that the use of cradleboards has an impact on the psychological development of children.[7]

Nigeria: The Restraint of Hausa Mothers

Parents, even in malarial places like northwestern Nigeria, where the risk of infant death is high, have concerns beyond the survival or health of their babies. As we mentioned in the introduction, Sarah first encountered this while observing Hausa-Fulani mothers there who avoided face-to-face contact with their infants when breast-feeding. This looked like "maternal deprivation" to Sarah, who had been trained as a child therapist. The Hausa practice is derived from a code called *kunya,* whose foremost stricture is that a wife should not utter her husband's name; at the local clinic, a woman had to take along an older child to tell the clerk her husband's family name. The Hausa-Fulani mothers understood *kunya* to ban eye contact, play, or talk in their infant care. Many of their children would also be sent away for fostering by kin after weaning (during the second year) and might not see their mothers for years.

Kunya is a serious matter; it means "shame" or "embarrassment," but also moral worth. To maintain your status as a moral person, you must abide by the rules, at least in public. It is related to a broader code of emotional restraint in the face of pain and adversity (called *filako*) that has given Hausa-Fulani women the reputation of never crying out during labor when they give birth in hospitals. By the time a young woman becomes a mother, she is thoroughly imbued with these rules as personal standards. Sarah's observations of individual mothers revealed how *kunya* affects the infant's social life:

Indo's first child, a daughter named Umma, was eleven months old when I first observed her. Indo had been married at fifteen and was only eighteen when we met. As the fourth and newest wife of Alhaji Abu, she was assigned much of the work in a compound with close to twenty residents, and she rarely had a chance to rest. Meanwhile, little Umma was actively cared for by Indo's co-wives, and she played with one or more of her dozen or so half-brothers and sisters living in the compound.

During many hours in her company, I never saw or heard Indo break the avoidance rule. If while sweeping, washing clothes or preparing food, she found herself in Umma's vicinity and the child reached out to her, Indo would hurry away. If she sat to shell beans on the veranda and Umma crawled over to her, she would set the little girl between her legs and balance her there facing *outwards* while she went on with her task. If Umma cried and the other children were unable to distract her, Indo would give her the breast; but if Umma reached up to caress her face,

Indo didn't look down. Out in the yard, she would speak when another adult spoke to her but she didn't initiate conversation; in short, she behaved according to the rules prescribed for a "bride" and a young mother, low in the household hierarchy.

Indo's sudden vivacity with Umma on the rare occasion I was alone with them in Indo's own small room was in sharp contrast with her reserve out in the compound. It emerged that she had four years of schooling, enjoyed reading storybooks and had plenty to tell me about her life before marriage. But although she held Umma more in the privacy of her own room than she did out in the yard, she was no more affectionate. When I asked her why she didn't talk to her small daughter, with a puzzled look she replied, "Why talk to child before she's learned how to talk?"

At some point when Umma was between eighteen and twenty-two months, Alhaji Abu would decide it was time for her to be weaned. Then Indo would take her to her own mother who lived in another town. "My mother has told me she wants my daughter, and so, after a few days, when Umma asks for the breast I'll refuse her. I'll leave her and come back here, and unless her father wants her with him here in town, she may stay with my mother till she marries."

"You won't have any say in the matter?" I asked.

"Saratu, don't you know that where a child lives and with whom is up to the father?"

The impact of *kunya* restrictions on mother-infant interaction is situational: the more public the setting in her husband's compound, the more likely a mother is to avoid face-to-face interaction with her baby, while she feels freer in her parents' compound. Even when the child is not her firstborn, however, she may be far less engaging with her child than other people in the compound. Sarah observed each of nineteen babies with their mothers three times over a period of seven months and spent extra time with a number of them.[8] She found that there were on average three to four adult women in the compound who responded rapidly to a baby's cry or call for interaction, especially when the mother herself was inhibited by *kunya*. The women of the compound thus acted as collective backup for the mother, permitting her to restrain her social interaction.

Not only are these infant care practices of the Hausa-Fulani mothers unfamiliar to Americans, but they also seem irrational, arbitrary, and burdensome. Surely parents in our own society, driven as we are by concern for the infant in a practical context, would not let irrational feelings stand in the way of interacting sensibly with our offspring. Or would we?

How Shall I Feed My Baby?

For the first 200,000 years of human existence, mothers did not have to ask this question, though some engaged other women to breast-feed their babies. Then, in 1867, Justus von Liebig, a pioneering German chemist (the founder of organic chemistry and the "father of the fertilizer industry"), devised a synthetic formula to replace breast milk for infants. Liebig's Soluble Food for Babies was soon being produced and used in England and the United States, particularly among urban middle- and upper-class (nonworking) women influenced by medical doctors. From the 1870s onwards, there was experimentation with different—largely inadequate—formulas designed to nourish babies and reduce infant mortality. They could not prevent mortality, since they did not address its source—the deadly bacterial infections to which infants are susceptible—but the use of formula in bottles as a means of feeding babies nevertheless caught on; it fit the Victorian morality of the time. Bottle-feeding brought about

a long-term change in the way Westerners think and feel about
infant care. As increasing numbers of mothers adopted the bottle, breast-feeding became a source of shame, and many mothers even avoided talking about it until at least the 1960s. In 1952
a Boston-area mother explained her choice to an interviewer:
"I didn't want to feed him any other way [than the bottle], and I
felt that breast-feeding was done in privacy or within your own
home, not in front of anyone, and you could never tell when anyone might walk in unexpectedly. I guess I am pretty modest in
that respect, but I didn't want anyone to see me."[9]

When Bob read this excerpt to a group of mostly female
university students in Nigeria, he saw their puzzlement turn to
amusement and then to consternation: How could a mother be
embarrassed by feeding her baby the way all mothers do? What
was wrong with this mother who thought nursing her baby in
isolation was a sign of modesty? Did all Americans feel that way?
Bob pointed out that in this Boston-area survey in 1951–1952, 60
percent of mothers did not breast-feed their babies at all, and
another 24 percent ended their breast-feeding before the baby
was three months old. By contrast, all Yoruba mothers in urban
western Nigeria (where Bob was teaching at that time) breast-
fed their babies on average for almost two years; a stroll down
any street or marketplace quickly revealed that breast-feeding in
public drew no attention from onlookers and caused no anxiety
to mothers. The students listened with widening eyes to Bob's
explanation about the erotic significance of the female breast in
American popular culture, but they remained appalled at the per-
versity of women who could confuse a mother's nurturance with
something shameful to be concealed from others.

American and British mothers in the mid-twentieth century
often reported that they were *unable* to breast-feed. The Boston
survey found that 26 percent of the mothers said they could not

nurse their babies. In England a few years later, mothers who gave birth in a hospital or at home with a midwife were under official pressure to breast-feed, and most did so for at least a few days. The psychologists John and Elizabeth Newson surveyed 709 mothers in Nottingham during 1959–1960 and found that four days after birth, when most remained in the hospital, 83 percent of the mothers were breast-feeding, "or at least still making some attempt to do so."[10] But after two weeks, when they were out of the hospital or the midwife had stopped her daily visits, the proportion still breast-feeding dropped to 60 percent, and by the time the baby was one month old only 54 percent of the mothers were breast-feeding. Why so few? The Newsons considered the possibility that employment was the reason but found that hardly any of the mothers were working. Most of the Nottingham mothers who had not breast-fed or had given up early claimed, like their American counterparts, that they were *physically unable* to breast-feed.

The Newsons, like the researchers in Boston, concluded that shame about exposing the breast, stemming from its significance as a sex symbol, was the underlying reason for the avoidance of breast-feeding and that the mothers found it embarrassing to admit to feeling ashamed, hence their claims of physical inadequacy. In other words, these British and American mothers of the mid-twentieth century, like the Hausa-Fulani mothers in northern Nigeria, had rather complicated moral feelings that affected the care they gave their infants.

Breast-feeding and the Bottle in America

The squeamishness of American and British mothers about breast-feeding in the 1950s was a cultural legacy of the late nineteenth century. The historian Jill Lepore tells us of a reported "American epidemic of lactation failure" as early as 1887.[11]

Doctors recommended breast-feeding to mothers, but they were Victorian-era men, and their avoidance of touching the breast apparently rendered them ineffective in helping mothers get started. Thus, women began to see themselves as unable to feed their babies from their breasts.[12]

Those who preferred the bottle did not have jobs that took them outside the home but based their preference on feelings of shame or disgust aroused by what had been a normal human practice (and remained so in most agrarian societies). There is no way of explaining this historical change without taking into account the taboos regarding sexual display in the Victorian culture of late-nineteenth-century and early-twentieth-century America and Britain.

Cultural influences, however, can be reversed. By the late 1960s and early 1970s—almost a century after the decline in breast-feeding began—American and British mothers, now influenced by a new code of "natural" motherhood and an invigorated medical consensus favoring breast-feeding, were beginning to change in the opposite direction. Whereas the Boston-area survey of 1952 found that 60 percent of the mothers did not breast-feed at all, by 2008 the proportion who did not breast-feed in Massachusetts as a whole had declined to 23.1 percent, roughly the same as the US national average. In other words, more than 70 percent of mothers in Massachusetts and the United States as a whole now initiated breast-feeding, and 44.3 percent were still breast-feeding, though not exclusively, at six months.[13] And once again, this trend cannot be explained by employment, since the proportion of mothers of young children who worked had increased greatly over the same period that breast-feeding was increasing—that is, since 1970.[14] The struggle to return to breast-feeding was won by medical experts persuading an increasing number of mothers that the health of their babies required that they be breast-fed.

All of this goes to show that infant care, however rooted in the human genome, can be influenced by cultural ideologies, technologies, information, and expert advice to mothers, all of which vary over time and across cultures.

While American and British women were concerning themselves with whether they were able to breast-feed—or wanted to—during the late nineteenth and early twentieth centuries, women in most of the agrarian world went on doing what humans had always done: feeding their infants at the breast, often without imagining any alternative. Only women in the more affluent countries and in rapidly urbanizing Latin America had the possibility of choice. We say the *possibility* of choice because their actual choices reflected the pressure of their peers and the medical experts.

In two generations, from 1950 to 2000, the American population changed from one in which a majority of mothers did *not* breast-feed at all to one in which 70 percent initiated breast-feeding—by 2011 it was 79 percent. A new conception of infant care, with a greater emphasis on mother-infant affection and interaction, was taking hold. Yet these two generations became parents under different conditions. Sarah experienced the first period, beginning in 1964, when she was an unmarried social work student working in a residential treatment center for children:

Sarah was watching one of the children from the center make mud pies in the sandbox of a Chicago park when a woman whose son was playing in the same sandbox, said, "Your daughter's cute. Did you nurse her?" Sarah confessed (without revealing that this was not her child) that she had not, and the woman declared, "Well, make sure you nurse your next child!" And identifying herself as a member of La Leche League, she launched into a lecture on breast-feeding, which was uncommon at the time. But by 1970, when Sarah gave birth to Anna, two of her close friends, who had not breast-fed their older children, had recently given birth again and were assiduously breast-feeding their new babies. With their encouragement (and ointment for sore nipples), Sarah followed suit. She laid in six bottles with a special pot in which to decontaminate them and a store of milk formula should her efforts falter, but they didn't. When Anna turned one month, her pediatrician suggested that Sarah begin giving her a teaspoonful of cereal "to encourage her to sleep through the night." (On a "full" stomach, by six weeks she was obligingly sleeping from 11:00 PM to 4:00 AM.) Sarah introduced the first Gerber baby food, apple sauce, at three months, and at six months "finger food." By the time she lost interest in nursing at nine months, Anna was eating "regular food" and drinking cow's milk from a cup she held herself. Aside from sips of water, she had never drunk anything from a bottle. (Since Sarah didn't work outside the home while she was nursing, she never touched her store of formula.)

In the next generation—that is, after the 1970s—an increasing number of mothers worked full-time outside the home, which complicated their choice of feeding. They could have had substitute caretakers (nannies, home day care, or day care centers) give their babies synthetic milk formula in bottles, but they were more convinced (or pressured by the authority of experts to believe) that breast milk was best. Thus, their choice was to stay home and risk the loss of their jobs (since the United States does not legally mandate paid parental leave) or, after 1991, get a breast pump so that others could feed their babies. The burdens of mothering multiplied. Satisfying the demands of the medical experts for breast-feeding (or at least feeding breast milk) and those of employers for work could be stressful. And there were no readily available compromise solutions for the potential conflicts; mothers felt that they were on their own in meeting these demands. If mothers did opt for breast pumps, what about the affection and interaction that had previously accompanied breast-feeding?

Breast-feeding and Risky Infant Care in Africa

The vast majority of mothers living south of the Sahara breast-feed, despite efforts by commercial firms since the 1970s to introduce synthetic milk formula. Does that mean that all of their traditional practices were adaptive, in the sense of diminishing risks to the survival of their infants? On the contrary, risky practices like denying colostrum to the newborn and the force-feeding of gruel (as well as the killing of twins and the giving of daily enemas to infants) were found in various parts of the sub-Saharan region.

Colostrum is the watery fluid produced by a mother's breasts late in pregnancy and in the immediate postnatal period, before the milk comes in. It rehydrates the newborn without exposure to infection, has a laxative effect that cleans out toxic waste, and, most importantly, provides immunity to infection, especially in the first day after birth. Yet in many hunting-gathering and agrarian societies, including those in Africa, customary practices delay breast-feeding for one to seven days, thus denying the newborn the better chances for survival that come from colostrum feeding.

Force-feeding of gruel was practiced in East and West Africa before bottles with rubber nipples became widely available. The mother would block her baby's nostrils with her hand and then, as the child gasped for air, pour the liquid into his mouth. The mother intended for the infant to swallow only some of the gruel, but the rest would be initially inhaled, causing the baby to spit up to clear his airways. Bob once witnessed a Yoruba mother in western Nigeria force-feed her baby, who choked and sputtered for a few minutes. It was frightening to watch and seemed to endanger the child's life. But it had been practiced daily among the Gusii in Kenya (in the past) and many other African peoples, not only by mothers but also by other caretakers. Like colostrum denial, force-feeding *elevates* the risks of infant mortality among people already inhabiting a high-risk environment. We cannot explain why these practices were widespread, but we note that they were clearly maladaptive and tended—along with dietary regimes that led to malnutrition—to refute any simple notion that folk knowledge and practice are generally adaptive or beneficial to children.[15] Yes, the Gusii kangaroo maternal care for preterm infants and Mayan midwives' massage to prevent breech births, as described in the previous chapter, are examples of beneficial practices that probably saved the lives of babies and mothers alike, but the beneficence of these examples cannot be extrapolated to folk practices in general.

African mothers nonetheless breast-feed their babies, not because they believe it to be healthier or more natural than the bottle, but as the necessary centerpiece around which other aspects of infant care—especially the management of sleep and crying—have always been organized. Most African babies are breast-fed for a long time—between one and three years—but the duration varies by region, and it has also been changing, mostly toward shorter durations as African women go to school, gain income, and move to cities. In many African societies, a woman must avoid sexual relations until she has weaned her child, often because of a belief that semen poisons breast milk. In others, weaning may be delayed until the new pregnancy is visible. Sarah never saw a mother in any of the communities in which she worked nursing a toddler after the birth of his younger sibling. She was told that if a mother were to do so, the older child's feeding would poison the milk for his follower.

How Do I Sleep After Giving Birth?

One common answer of American parents is: you don't—not until the baby *sleeps through the night,* whenever that may be. Exhaustion due to sleeplessness is the common experience that young parents talk about during this period. They complain, not only because everyone hates to be awakened repeatedly at night, but also because the exhaustion interferes with their work the next day, and there is no end to it in sight. Moreover, babies continue to wake up their parents at least occasionally long after they first sleep through the night. But since it's inevitable, parents have no choice but to endure this grueling experience. Or do they?

The exhaustion of American parents of newborn children results in part from a standard arrangement in the household (also found in much of western Europe) in which babies sleep separately from their parents, not only in a crib (cot) separated from the parental bed but in a room of their own. The mother is not close enough to the infant for easy breast-feeding, and both mother and father are too far away to respond rapidly to the baby's cry. Since infants do tend to cry for food and comfort, the arrangement is guaranteed to make parental response burdensome and, eventually, exhausting. Why do parents arrange things this way? The short answer is that they think it's in the child's best interest: not only are the risks of having the baby in the bed with them eliminated, but the newborn is provided with a pathway to future independence (a value central to both British and American culture). The longer answer involves the insistent claims of pediatricians and psychiatrists that co-sleeping endangers the child's survival and future mental health. We consider the evidence for that claim later in the chapter, but first let's take a quick look around the world.

Co-sleeping Versus Isolation

Agrarian peoples throughout Asia, Africa, Latin America, and the Pacific sleep with their babies. And in Japan—a large, modern country—parents universally sleep with their infants, yet their infant mortality rate is one of the lowest in the world—2.8 deaths per 1,000 live births versus 6.2 in the United States—and their rate of SIDS (sudden infant death syndrome) is roughly half the US rate.[16] The Japanese case alone should make us suspect that the danger attributed to mother-infant co-sleeping in the United States has been exaggerated.

The biological anthropologist James McKenna has long advocated (and investigated) mother-child co-sleeping, from early infancy onwards, as a practice that evolved with humans and was almost universal among agrarian peoples. McKenna, who directs the Mother-Baby Sleep Laboratory at the University of Notre Dame, has provided detailed evidence of the physiological synchronization between mother and infant when they sleep together, especially when they start early and are breast-feeding, and of the safety features built into the practice—as opposed to the standard practice of putting the baby to sleep in a crib in another room.[17]

But McKenna's views are opposed by the pediatric establishment. The American Academy of Pediatrics declared a policy against co-sleeping (they call it "bed-sharing") in 2005 and reinforced it with further specifications in 2011. The pediatricians' emphasis is entirely on *safety*. They don't trust mothers to arrange themselves and their children safely in bed, whereas a separate crib can be required to meet certified standards of manufacture. They are reluctant to admit any benefits from co-sleeping. However, the 2011 technical report of the Academy's Task Force on SIDS made a surprising admission:

> Parent-infant bed-sharing is common. In one national survey, 45% of parents responded that they had shared a bed with their infant (8 months of age or younger) at some point in the preceding two weeks. In some racial/ethnic groups, the rate of routine bed-sharing might be higher. . . .
>
> Parent-infant bed-sharing continues to be controversial. Although electrophysiologic and behavioral studies [by McKenna] have offered a strong case for its effect in facilitating breastfeeding, and although many parents believe that they can maintain vigilance of the infant while they are asleep and bed-sharing, epidemiologic studies have shown that bed-sharing can be hazardous under certain conditions.[18]

Those conditions include parents smoking in bed and exposure to the risk of "accidental injury and death, such as suffocation, asphyxia, entrapment, falls, and strangulation."[19] These risks are also associated with poverty, alcoholism, and smoking, suggesting to us (though not to the American Academy of Pediatrics) that co-sleeping *by itself* is not harmful.

The many studies of Western parents, from California to Norway, who sleep with their children have looked for pathological or problematic outcomes. Overall, hardly any such outcomes have been found. Some surveys found parent-child co-sleeping to be correlated with the "sleep disturbance" of children, but close examination revealed that often the situation was not that bed-sharing had caused children's sleep disturbance, but the reverse: children had been taken into the parental bed *because* they weren't sleeping well.

What about the claim that co-sleeping undermines the child's independence? American parents want their babies to get off to a good start by sleeping in their own beds rather than picking up the "bad habits" that might come from sleeping with their parents. This was the expert advice of pediatricians at the outset of the twentieth century, based on a mixture of concerns about hygiene and American individualism. After World War II, the prominent pediatricians Benjamin Spock and T. Berry Brazelton were influenced by psychoanalysis and tended to give the same advice, for somewhat different reasons. In classical Freudian theory, there is the danger that through the "primal scene" the infant or toddler witnessing the parents' sexual intercourse will be somehow traumatized and become mentally ill.[20] The psychologist Paul Okami has reviewed and analyzed research on exposure to parental nudity and sexual intercourse:

> Surprisingly then—especially considering the vehemence with which these behaviors have been condemned in much of the clinical literature—there is little evidence to support dire predictions. In the case of exposure to parental nudity, the very scant available evidence points to generally neutral or perhaps even positive correlates, particularly for boys. In the case of . . . primal scene experiences, the data indicate that adolescents or peripubertal children may react with displeasure to such experiences, younger children may react with amusement or noncomprehension. In any event, no empirical evidence links such experiences with subsequent psychological harm.[21]

Okami then analyzed the eighteen-year follow-up data on California children born in 1975 in the Family Lifestyles Project of the anthropologist Thomas Weisner, comparing countercultural ("hippie") families with the children of conventional two-parent families. Examining the outcomes at ages six and eighteen of those who were exposed to parental nudity and the primal scene, he again found no clear signs of pathology:

> Given virtually no evidence in this or any other empirical study that the behaviors examined in the current study are unambiguously harmful, the question becomes: Why is it so widely believed in the United States and certain European nations that these practices are uniformly detrimental to the mental health of children? . . . Such notions . . . are perhaps better conceptualized as *myths.*[22]

In a later widespread version of psychoanalysis that combined Freudian theory with American individualism, co-sleeping would be viewed as blocking the "separation-individuation" process and leading to the child's becoming "symbiotic" with—that is, pathologically overdependent on—the mother.[23] In other words, parents co-sleeping with their children are not only preventing their acquisition of independent habits but also endangering their mental health. Why take those risks? Neither Spock nor Brazelton could bring himself to advocate it.

Mother-Infant Interdependence in Japan

The anthropologist William Caudill, who observed Japanese mothers and infants sleeping together in the early 1960s, believed that the practice promoted the psychological "*inter*dependence" of the child and mother, but he claimed that such interdependence was not pathological but cultural—that such interdependence was normal in a Japanese context.[24] Many years later, an American scholar of Japan, Christine Gross-Loh, raised her own children in Tokyo, and her insightful 2013 book, *Parenting Without Borders,* contains the best discussion of the subject. She describes a ten-year-old named Tomo as a "mature, reliable, independent kid during the day" who "shared sleep with an adult at night."

> Japan is full of kids like Tomo. After years of living there on and off, my husband and I (and even our kids) have noticed that most children—the same children who sleep with their parents every night—take care of themselves and their belongings, work out peer conflicts, and show mature social behavior and self-regulation at a young age. Japanese parents expect their kids to be independent by taking care of themselves and being socially responsible. They expect them to help contribute to the household or school community by being capable and self-reliant.[25]

This does not sound like the pathology we would have expected from the (antiquated) psychoanalytic perspective. All things considered, we have to agree with McKenna's conclusion: the proven benefits of mother-infant co-sleeping far outweigh the largely imaginary risks. Putting a baby in a separate room at night is a Euroamerican cultural practice that burdens parents and leads to their exhaustion without guaranteeing the safety or future character development of their children.

That is our conclusion as anthropologists, but the debate over co-sleeping continues in the pediatric journals. In 2016 McKenna published an article in *Acta Paediatrica* that offers the new concept of "breastsleeping" to indicate the connection—in human evolution as well as for optimal health—between breast-feeding and co-sleeping.[26]

Co-sleeping and Sex in India, the United States, and Mexico

For parents, however, cultural practices like sleeping arrangements are not experiments to discover what works and what does not; they're more like moral codes to be followed. This is what the anthropologist Richard Shweder claimed after comparing the preferred sleeping arrangements of Hindu parents in Orissa (Odiya), India, with those of Chicago parents.[27] The Indian parents were open to a variety of arrangements in which children and babies slept with one parent or the other, but not the Chicagoans, who were primarily concerned with defending what Shweder calls the "sacred couple," that is, the husband and wife sleeping together. Their protectiveness of the marital alliance has to be reckoned as an element in the cultural practice. American parents give priority to maintaining the husband-wife relationship in bed; sleeping with the baby they love could be experienced as an intrusion on their primary relationship—with each other.

The priorities of parents in agrarian and transitional societies are quite different. In a small town in central Mexico, Sarah knew a couple—both university-educated—who lived in a house with three bedrooms but slept in the same room with their three children. The mother slept with her daughter and infant son, and the father in another bed with the older son. When they wanted to have sex, the husband would put the older son in the mother's bed with his siblings, and the wife would come into his bed. This arrangement might seem cumbersome to Americans (not to mention potentially "traumatic" to the children), but something like it is standard in most agrarian societies. Agrarian parents report finding it unproblematic, and they enjoy the convenience of having the breast-feeding baby in bed—as well as the body contact.

Infant care practices of feeding and sleeping can only be understood from the parents' point of view in the context of their other practices—or more accurately, in terms of their cultural ideals for maternal care *as a whole,* as implemented in their observable behavior. This chapter has shown some of the burdens that American parents, guided by pediatric experts, impose on themselves for questionable ends.

Next we examine how African mothers compare with their Western counterparts on emotional interaction. In Chapter 5, we turn to other parts of the agrarian world.

∾ 4 ∾

Mother and Infant:
Face-to-Face or Skin-to-Skin?

FOR AMERICANS, expressing "affection" to babies in word and deed is natural, automatic, and entirely positive. For a mother not to be affectionate with her own baby is inconceivable and possibly reprehensible. What kind of a mother would *withhold* affection from her own infant? Perhaps she's clinically depressed! It's hard for us to imagine that the maternal behavior we consider affectionate could be seen rather differently in other cultures—as disrespectful, dangerously boastful, or overexciting to the infant. Yet different codes of emotional expression endow our "affection" with varied meanings, requiring restraint where we would be expressive.

The United States and
Western Societies: Face to Face

What we Westerners mean by affection in infant care is shown in the photo insert by an American mother interacting with her

67

baby. Theirs is, first and foremost, a face-to-face interaction: the mother's facial expressions are displayed to the baby, and the latter's face is fully visible to the mother. Their eye contact or mutual gaze is a key component, perhaps the most emotionally arousing part, of their interaction, but the mother's smile—intended to elicit a reciprocal smile from the baby—is also important. She responds quickly to any of the infant's motions or facial expressions, hoping to encourage a contingent, back-and-forth reciprocity in which an act on one side triggers action from the other.

From a comparative perspective, another important part of this cultural practice is that it takes place *at a distance,* usually without touching, sometimes with objects like toys, and with much talking by the mother intended to excite the baby to more and more positive arousal. Thus, the face-to-face mother-infant interaction as a Euroamerican cultural practice involves eye contact, smiling and other distal (nontouching) displays of emotion, contingency, talking, toys or other objects, and the goal of infant arousal.

Africa: Skin to Skin

For African mothers, breast-feeding and body contact, not face-to-face interaction, are the organizing features of infant care. Babies are often held on the mother's lap or legs facing in the same direction as the mother, and the contingencies of their interaction may not be readily apparent. But observations show that mothers do respond contingently, and rapidly, to infant crying with breast-feeding, jiggling, or changing the child's position on the mother's body. The amount a mother speaks to the baby varies, but her speaking is not central to the interaction and is distinctly infrequent by Western standards. The mother, instead of intending to arouse, tries to keep the baby calm. The American anthropologist Walter Goldschmidt, examining his photographs of this kind of mother-child interaction, termed Sebei mothers of Uganda "emotionally absent" with their infants, but Relindis Yovsi, an infant psychologist from Cameroon studying mothers and infants among her own Nso people, called it "responsive control."[1]

We need to look beyond those aspects of the American pattern that seem to be missing in the African pattern to include the daily, routine conditions of the African infant's life and the goals of her mother in an agrarian society. The infant in the picture sleeps at the mother's breast at night and spends much of the daytime on the mother's body or on the back of a sibling caregiver. Breast-feeding continues throughout the first year and beyond and is rapidly deployed in response to infant crying whenever the mother is available. In other words, tactile or skin-to-skin contact is almost continuous—a major contrast with the life of an American infant who sleeps apart from the mother and others. There are no toys or other objects to engage the baby in play; these African mothers want to keep their infants calm rather than excite them with extended episodes of mutual gaze, smiling, and talking. Their goal is a compliant baby, oriented to people rather than objects, who will become a respectful toddler and, later, an obedient child—once again, in contrast with the stated goals of American mothers. Differing goals and different strategies lead to dissimilar conditions for infant growth and development.

When Nso mothers in a focus group were told that in Germany babies sleep apart from their mothers, they refused to believe it—maltreatment of that kind could not be so widespread! Were it true, they said, they might have to send an Nso mother to Germany to convince the Germans they should stop it.[2]

This reaction reveals that the emotional involvement of a mother who sleeps with her infant and keeps the baby on her body for much of the daytime is not expressed through easily observed dramatic episodes like the mother-infant mock conversations we are used to in the West. Instead, it is built into the functional routines of infant care and openly expressed only when mothers contemplate violations of routine standards of skin-to-skin contact. Instead of being "emotionally absent" because they don't demonstrate their affection the way American and German mothers do, these mothers are emotionally *present* most of the time but expressing it differently, through reliable, unremitting, tactile care. A fine-grained analysis of observations made by Heidi Keller and her colleagues during the first twelve weeks after birth showed that contingent, back-and forth interaction increased among *both* German and Nso babies, but the German mothers maintained longer periods of face-to-face interaction than the Nso mothers, and the German babies increased in mutual gaze with their mothers over the first three months after birth, whereas the Nso babies did not.[3] This suggests that the cultural style of mothering affects very young babies. And indeed, the Nso children in the second year of life are more compliant and obedient than their German counterparts, in accord with their mothers' goals, a point we shall discuss in later chapters.

Results from the Nso-German comparison are consistent with what we found when we compared Gusii infant care with that of middle-class American mothers, despite the fact that the Nso live in the West African country of Cameroon and the Gusii are thousands of miles away in the East African country of Kenya. But Nso and Gusii are both agrarian peoples, just as the Germans of Muenster and the Americans of Boston are modern, Western, urban, postindustrial peoples, and that shows in their styles of infant care.

Stimulating Versus Soothing

We spent two years studying the infant care of the Gusii, high-land farmers of southwestern Kenya, and later compared their practices with those of middle-class Americans. In our project, which involved pediatricians and other physicians as well as anthropologists, we observed twenty-eight Gusii infants and their mothers for the first thirty months—that is, from birth until the infants were two and a half years old—and we observed twenty middle-class American mothers and their babies at home in the Boston area.[4]

We found many differences between Gusii and American parents in their conceptions of what infants need, how they develop, and how they should be prepared for life. Gusii mothers rarely told us explicitly their goals or strategies for infant care; we often had to reconstruct their perspective from many hours of observing them at home, carried out by Sarah and our team of Gusii and American observers, as well as by interviewing them. Much of Gusii mothers' infant care can be described as *soothing*. They sought to keep their babies calm and quiet by holding them on their bodies, or giving them to older siblings to hold, day and night; by responding rapidly to their frets and cries, but rarely to their undistressed babbles; by breast-feeding frequently and on demand; and, when we put their babies in an infant seat for face-to-face interaction, by turning away when the baby became positively excited. They did not use toys or other objects to play with or excite their infants.

The American mothers held their babies much less—about half as much at three months and one-fourth as much at nine months of age. The Americans talked to their infants more than twice as much at three and six months and about two and a half times as much at nine months, and they also tolerated far more crying—more than twice as much at three months. We say "tolerated" because when we showed some of the Gusii mothers a video of an American mother diapering a six-week-old who was crying on the changing table, they clearly found it intolerable and protested the neglect they saw in letting an infant cry *even for a few seconds* without immediate bodily contact.

Yet the Gusii mothers' reactions, and their soothing practices, do not reflect what Americans call an "indulgent" attitude. Gusii mothers can be verbally harsh with babies who step out of line with their expectations of compliance, and most rarely kiss their babies or give them what we would consider signs of affection or love. Furthermore, they believe that infants should learn *fear* for their own protection from hazards, and they sometimes try to frighten an older whimpering baby by pretending to call a dog: "Aso, aso, esese."[5] Most importantly, they do not consider providing the infant with continuous skin-to-skin contact (with themselves or child caregivers) or their rapid responses to infant crying (including breast-feeding day and night) to be "indulging" the baby's desires or impulses. For Gusii mothers, the practices we have called "soothing" are the minimal obligations of a competent mother implementing Gusii standards of infant care. From their perspective, this is sensible and decent, not emotionally indulgent, behavior.

The American mothers, on the other hand, were explicit about wanting to stimulate and excite their infants when they were awake rather than keep them calm and soothed. They believed that babies *need* stimulation for their mental and social development, as well as exciting interaction with their mothers to build an essential relationship. When looking at and talking to their babies, they expressed affection and overtly took pleasure in these social contacts, even though they held and fed the infants less than the Gusii did.

"Indulgence," then, like "affection," "warmth," and "emotional security," is in the eye of the observer. These terms are packed with our own cultural and theoretical assumptions and don't travel well across cultures. In other words, calling Gusii infant care "indulgent" not only misattributes to Gusii mothers an emotional attitude from our own culture that can, but need not, accompany soothing behavior but also injects a speculative Freudian implication of gratification or overgratification. Should we call Gusii mothers "coldly indulgent" or "unaffectionately indulgent"? We prefer to call their behavior soothing and assume that maternal behavior can be accompanied by differing emotional attitudes and intentions in different cultures.

The Gusii-US contrast and the Nso-German contrast reflect in part the different agendas of African and Western mothers. The Gusii, for example, want a calm infant and a compliant child, and they use soothing to achieve those aims; Americans want an emotionally engaged, active, and independent child, and they stimulate and arouse the infant toward those ends. Young American children at thirty months of age seem to be far more active, talkative, and unruly than their Gusii counterparts, who (like the Nso) are more compliant, so it seems clear that both sets of mothers are successful in achieving their own cultural goals for early (behavioral) development—a point we shall consider again in later chapters.

Gusii and American infant care practices also reflect the different demographic contexts in which mothers raise their children. For the average Gusii mother, who bears ten children, each child born is the primary focus of care only during the twenty-one months on average before the birth of the "follower." During that birth interval, she has to attend to the infant's survival in the face of significant challenges as well as prepare him as a toddler for entry into the group of older siblings, who act as a team to help the mother with domestic activities, including child care, so that she can tend to crop cultivation, food processing, and market trade. One sibling carries the baby on her back when the mother is working, and the team later absorbs the toddler as an apprentice in acquiring skills in communication, household tasks, and the care of domestic animals.

In contrast with their quick responsiveness to their infants' crying, Gusii mothers are relatively *unresponsive* to their infants' babbles or attempts at eye contact in the second half of the first year. We found Gusii mothers responding verbally to infant babbling ("non-distress vocalizations") at nine to ten months only 5 percent of the time, while the American mothers responded verbally 20 percent of the time. Only 1 percent of Gusii mothers' acts toward their infants at nine to ten months involved looking, while looking was involved in 43 percent of the American mothers' acts. The Boston mothers looked at their infants at this age more than three times as frequently (28 percent of the time) as the infants looked at them (8 percent), while the Gusii mothers looked at their infants about the same amount (9 percent) as the infants looked at them. We often watched Gusii mothers holding babies facing outward in their laps in a social situation without ever looking at or talking to the baby; they also moved the baby around for breast-feeding while continuing a conversation with another mother—again, without looking at or talking to the baby. They obviously did not see breast-feeding as an opportunity for social interaction with the infant. Talking accounted for 29 percent of the Boston mothers' acts toward their nine- to ten-month-olds, but for only 11 percent of the Gusii mothers' acts.[6] These dramatic differences in frequency reveal a different set of assumptions about what infants need and how an "ordinary devoted mother" (in the words of the English psychoanalyst-pediatrician D. W. Winnicott) should satisfy those needs.[7] Sarah's observations reveal how Gusii mothers shared a code of conduct but also varied among themselves in actual behavior:

> I observed Justin, the fifth child of Charles and Marisera (who would ultimately bear seven children), first when he was six weeks old and then at three-month intervals until shortly after his first birthday. Relations between his parents—his father worked 500 miles away on the Kenya coast, only came home every two years or so and between times rarely sent money—were strained, a not uncommon situation in a community in which a majority of fathers worked "outside." Justin lived with his thirty-year-old mother and siblings (aged four through thirteen) in a large homestead headed by his paternal grandfather. Marisera, for whom Charles had paid a (large) bride-price of fourteen head of cattle, was appreciated by her in-laws for her hard work and the four sons she had borne, the oldest of whom was already thirteen. Despite Charles's erratic performance as a husband, his parents were committed to her and willing to provide the material and social support that ought to have come from their son.
>
> Marisera, who had grown up a few miles away and had not attended school, was well liked in the community. In adult company, she had a bright social manner, but in her own house with her children or alone she seemed self-absorbed and depressed. As a young baby, Justin was almost always with his mother, who, however, aside from feeding and cleaning him, seemed to show little interest in him. Marisera's response to any sound he made, whether or not it indicated distress, was to offer him the breast. She never engaged in social interaction unless it was initiated by him. As the months passed, such episodes became rarer until, during a day-long observation and videotaping session when Justin was a year old and bright-eyed, Marisera evaded all but

a few seconds' eye contact with her son, despite his vigorous attempts to get her attention. Observing (and videotaping) this interaction, I found it painful to watch. Justin's sister Jane, his main *omoreri*, babysitter, did not play with him. When he cried she might nuzzle him briefly, but mostly she jiggled him or tried to feed him the gruel their mother had prepared before leaving for the fields or the beer drink. Other homestead residents (in all there were thirty-one) took only a cursory interest in Justin, and only his paternal grandmother and a two-year-old cousin played with him now and then.

Marisera seemed to be avoiding emotional contact with her little boy. But while her disengagement was a concern to me and other members of our research team, we never heard her friends and relatives criticize her behavior. She might not be as responsive as some other neighborhood women were to their infants, but she was raising a physically robust child. Therefore, from a Gusii perspective, she was an adequate mother.

On the other hand, there was Evans, whom Sarah observed at three-month intervals from nine to twenty-one months:

Evans was the second child of young parents. His father, twenty-seven-year-old Joshua, had some secondary schooling and was fluent in both Swahili and English; his mother, twenty-four-year-old Elizabeth, had five years of primary school and regularly read a Swahili newspaper. Joshua worked as a surveyor for a government agency and was home only at the weekend. Meanwhile Elizabeth kept their small house, with its European-style furniture, meticulously clean, and the grass in the yard neatly cut. A cheerfully energetic woman, Elizabeth dealt effectively with her quarrelsome in-laws and had already achieved more stature in the neighborhood than was usual for someone so junior in the local hierarchy. . . . She was hidden from the eyes of neighbors by a high hedge, and she delighted in entertaining and being entertained by her baby. Evans was the "follower" of four-year-old Paul. Elizabeth had no doubt played with Paul during his infancy just as she now played with Evans, and Paul was an unusually articulate child. So precocious was he that Elizabeth, worried he might provoke neighbors' jealousy and malevolence, tried her best to keep him at home. Whenever he slipped through the gate, she would fetch him back and punish him severely.

Although Elizabeth spent much of her time at home with the children, she also called upon two young sisters-in-law who had finished primary school and were "waiting" to get married to watch the children while she tended her fields. At nine months of age, Evans was clearly accustomed to receiving a good deal of attention from his mother, brother, aunts, and, when he was home, his father. As he got older, he would initiate games as often as they did. Yet, lively as he was, weaning at seventeen months (when Elizabeth was again pregnant) set him back. After crying for three days (so his mother reported to me), he was noticeably clingy, and though this anxious mood soon passed, now that his mother was out of the house more than she'd been when he was at the breast, the exuberant little boy with whom I was familiar was replaced by a much quieter child.

By Gusii standards, Elizabeth was an unusually playful mother. Despite her heavy domestic workload, she gave baby Evans a good deal of social as well as physical attention. Her more traditional neighbors might say it wasn't surprising Evans was so sad after weaning; hadn't Elizabeth been too playful? By behaving more like a grandmother than a mother, hadn't she raised Evans's expectations for social engagement, expectations that, once the new baby came, she wouldn't have time or energy to meet? On the other hand, the liveliness of his older brother Paul suggested that Evans's sadness and passivity, still discernible four months after weaning, might be just a transient phase. In time, mightn't he reach a new equilibrium and become as socially confident as Paul?

Africa: Affectionate Hunter-Gatherers

The hunting-gathering peoples of Africa are clearly less inhibited than agrarian East Africans like the Gusii in their codes and practices of emotional expression among adults, and that difference affects their infant care. The anthropologist Melvin Konner reported on the !Kung San of the Kalahari semi-desert in Botswana:

> When the mother is standing [with the baby in a sling and on her hip], the infant's face is just at the eye-level of desperately maternal 10- to 12-year-old girls who frequently approach and initiate brief, intense, face-to-face interactions, including mutual smiling and vocalization. When not in the sling they [the infants] are passed from hand to hand around a fire for similar interactions with one adult or child after another. They are kissed on their faces, bellies, genitals, sung to, bounced, entertained, encouraged, even addressed at length in conversational tones long before they can understand words. Throughout the first year there is rarely any dearth of such attention and love.

Concerning smiling, Konner reported that "by at least the second month people try repeatedly, with some success, to elicit social smiles by bouncing the infant or stroking his cheeks with simultaneous face-to-face interaction."[8]

Marjorie Shostak, in her book *Nisa*, reported similar interactions: "When the child is not in the sling, the mother may be amusing her—bouncing, singing, or talking. . . .!Kung fathers—indulgent, affectionate, and devoted—also form very intense mutual attachments with their children. . . . Fathers, like mothers, are not viewed as figures of awesome authority, and their relationships with their children are intimate, nurturant and physically close."[9] What these quotations and every other source of information we have seen about the !Kung San imply is that their pattern of interaction with babies is recognizably "affectionate" in American terms (though not identical to American practices). No observer has accused !Kung San parents of being "emotionally absent" with their babies!

The anthropologist Barry Hewlett reported that, among the forest-dwelling Aka hunter-gatherers of the Central African Republic, "parents interact with and stimulate their infants throughout the day. They talk to, play with, show affection to, and transmit subsistence skills to their infants during the day."[10] He also pointed out, however, that Aka is not a child-focused society, like the United States, but rather adult-centered in that parents do not stop an activity to pay undivided attention to an infant; nevertheless, children are permitted a great deal of autonomy from the beginning. The Aka are noted, as revealed through Hewlett's research, for the important role played by fathers in infant care; he showed that "mothers were most likely to provide nourishment and transport the infant, while fathers were more likely to hug, kiss, or clean the infant they were holding."[11] Overall, the Aka appear to be emotionally expressive with their infants in ways that we would characterize as "affectionate." We have no information from African hunter-gatherers suggesting the kind of emotional restraint or gaze aversion common among some African agrarian peoples.

West Africa

In the coastal forest region of West Africa, where a large proportion of the sub-Saharan population lives, agrarian peoples like the Beng of the Ivory Coast and the Yoruba of Nigeria also seem far less restrained with their children than we found in Kenya, yet hierarchical inhibitions may nevertheless haunt infant care. Unlike the Gusii and other peoples of eastern Africa whose scattered homesteads and mother-child households are isolated from each other, West Africans live in clustered villages and densely packed compounds where a gregarious bonhomie prevails. Positive emotions are publicly, constantly, and often noisily expressed, giving the impression of an uninhibited people, but the code has its own restraints. In the traditional Yoruba compound, for example, each son prostrates himself daily—forehead touching the floor—before the patriarch. This is only one of many hierarchical routines specific to Yoruba family life, though the Yoruba are extremely gregarious and raise babies in a recognizably "warm" interpersonal environment.

Among the Beng, for whom the anthropologist Alma Gottlieb provided a cultural account of infancy, babies are talked to a great deal (Beng believe that children are born from a preexisting spirit world and are thus able to understand any language) and experience face-to-face interaction with smiling and eye contact. But, Gottlieb noted, "Beng adults train even babies not to interrupt adults' speech because children are expected to show deference to their elders."[12] Thus, even in an agrarian context where adults are emotionally warm, outgoing, and verbal to babies, deference is required during the first year of life. Agrarian peoples in Africa vary widely in emotional expression, but they share a concern with status in the domestic hierarchy that affects mother-infant relations.

Mexico and Zambia

Sarah spent many hours videotaping Mexican mothers and their infants in the city of Cuernavaca in the 1980s and in Tilzapotla, a market town, in the early 1990s. She saw that mothers with little or no formal education rarely talked to their infants. (Like Hausa or Gusii mothers, they would say, "Why talk to a child before he's learned to talk?") Soon after, in Ndola, a copper-mining city in Zambia, where Sarah videotaped mothers with their infants and young children, she saw mothers behaving in ways already familiar to her from northern Nigeria, Kenya, and Mexico. These Zambian mothers, however, had all been to school (some had finished high school) and lived in modern cinder-block houses in a densely urban environment; they owned many consumer goods, and most were devout Christians and regular participants in church activities. Furthermore, in the multiethnic copper-belt environment, where sociability was highly valued, these women talked and gossiped with their neighbors all day long. Yet apart from giving their children orders ("Eat up!" to an infant, or "Fetch me that bucket!" to an older child), they rarely spoke to them.

Sarah concluded that in these Mexican and Zambian urban settings she was seeing recent migrants from the hinterland behaving like their own rural mothers had behaved toward them. In other words, though they were raising children in a radically different urban environment (and the Mexican mothers were raising two or three children rather than seven or eight) and had acquired skills in school, they behaved toward their children much as their agrarian mothers and grandmothers had: fostering compliance and obedience to enable the child to be easily absorbed into the household economy. They had not (yet) become what we have elsewhere called "pedagogical mothers":

The trend toward pedagogical mothering may be worldwide and is probably based on the increasing school experience of women, but it does not mean the end of cultural variations in parental practices of childhood experience. As Chavajay and Rogoff . . . have shown among the Mayans in Guatemala and as Fung . . . and Miller et al. . . . have shown in Taiwan, even mothers with high levels of schooling in those places behave differently toward their young children than their middle-class American counterparts, in ways reflecting their historical and cultural traditions.[13]

It also reflects whether they are first- or later-generation migrants from the countryside.

Comparing African Cultures: Gusii and Hausa

In the introduction, we noted that Sarah's concern at seeing the mother-infant avoidance motivated by *kunya* among the Hausa had been alleviated by getting to know Musa, a university student. Like many children she observed in northern Nigeria, Musa had been avoided by his mother in infancy and separated from her at weaning and yet had grown into a young man remarkably lacking in any signs of the social or emotional problems that might have been predicted by prevalent psychiatric theories of early development. The same was true of many Gusii and Mexican young people she came to know. Despite the fact that their busy mothers in agrarian contexts had not played with or stimulated them much in infancy, and that they'd had little intimate contact with their mothers after being weaned, in anticipation of the arrival of a younger sibling, they, like Musa, had grown into adults who showed no signs of intellectual deficit or emotional disturbance. This raises fundamental questions about parental influence during infancy that we consider in the final chapter.

Gusii mothers as a whole could be seen in terms of the Bowlby-Ainsworth attachment theory as not sufficiently "sensitive" to their infants' signals and thus as fostering "insecure attachment."[4] But this assumes that the Anglo-American way of communicating with a baby—reacting to infant signals at a distance by talking and looking—is optimal for his development and that the skin-to-skin interaction continuously provided by Gusii mothers, combined with their rapid (physical) responsiveness to infant crying, does not constitute a form of communication equally supportive of emotional security and attachment. Rather than leap to a conclusion skewed by our own culture's perspective, we prefer to assume that there are more forms of maternal sensitivity than have been imagined in attachment theory or captured by child development researchers.

Sarah's close observations revealed a difference between Hausa and Gusii mothers in their reasons for distancing themselves from their infants: Among the Hausa, a woman needed privacy to play with or even look at her baby in order to avoid the shame she would suffer if other women in the family saw her; she could be stigmatized as someone who lacked the moral sense embodied in the kin-avoidance conventions. Among the Gusii, a mother needed a hedge to protect her from the view of other women because she feared their jealousy, which could be elicited by announcing that she was pregnant, by overtly loving her baby "too much," or by having a verbally precocious child; in other words, any behavior revealing the pleasure she took in her children or drawing attention to her reproductive accomplishment could be interpreted as boasting and render her and her children vulnerable to the ill will (leading to witchcraft) of neighbors.

Thus, the restraints on face-to-face interaction between mother and infant in these two African cultures have different meanings, sources, and motives. A Hausa mother seeks to maintain the approval of the other women she counts on for support, whereas a Gusii mother is wary of the other women at home and in the neighborhood and counts on her own children for support.

From a contemporary American perspective, and even apart from attachment theory, the Gusii mother's single-minded focus on the physical care of her infant, rarely talking to or looking at the child, might seem like a form of emotional neglect. The assumption underlying such a judgment, like Sarah's reactions when she began her infant observations among the Hausa, is that we know babies everywhere need the kind of affection that contemporary Americans express to their infants and that African (Gusii, Sebei, Kipsigis, perhaps the Nso) infants are being deprived of it. But do we know that? Yes, if we listen to the psychiatrist John Bowlby, who claimed in 1953 that mother-love during infancy is as necessary to a baby's future mental health as vitamins are to her physical health. Sixty years later, however, this claim remains contested in developmental psychology, and findings from the rest of the world pose increasingly serious challenges to it.[15] There must be ways for American parents to view infant care in other cultures without imposing their own culture's judgments.

Emotional Expression in Infant Care

We know with certainty that there are different ways of expressing emotions, that cultures provide codes standardizing some of these ways as acceptable in parent-child contexts while stigmatizing others, and that observers imbued with one code (as we all are) can commit errors in interpreting behavior framed in a different code. When it comes to infant care, however, we

Westerners tend to believe that *our* standards for expressing emotion not only are preferable but have been discovered by science to be what all infants need to develop normally. Could we be overlooking the possibility that where standards for emotional expression differ from ours, infants may derive "emotional security" through touch and tactile contact rather than through talk and gaze? Or that, if it is indeed emotional security that all children need, it can be acquired after infancy and from interactions with persons other than the mother? In fact, many alternative possibilities have been overlooked by American and British psychiatrists and child psychologists. We need to look beyond their theories to examine further how parents of infants in other cultures express or restrain their emotions as they care for babies according to *their* standards.

Exciting Babies with Eye Contact

The meaning of eye contact is central to the cultural variations that have been observed. American mothers seek mutual gaze with their young babies, and Western researchers tend to be convinced that this emotionally arousing exchange is good for the infant's psychological development. Among peoples like the Gusii and Nso, however, mothers deliberately *avoid* eye contact with their babies. In fact, Nso mothers reported blowing into the faces of their infants looking at them, to avoid face-to-face contact, and claimed that they could not get work done if the child could not be easily taken care of by others.[16] In other words, they recognize that mutual gaze could build an exclusive (for them, undesirable) relationship with the mother. But eye contact between someone of lower status in the domestic hierarchy, including a baby, and someone higher, including the mother, is also coded in Gusii and Nso cultures as disrespectful. For a mother to engage her infant in eye contact would be to encourage the baby's development of disrespectful habits and thwart one of her cherished goals as a parent: to promote respect as a moral good in the context of a hierarchical family. Modern Western parents, on the other hand, in seeking an egalitarian relationship with their babies, *reduce* the status differential between parent and child and shape their own behavior to fit the infant's inclinations. They make eye contact with their babies because they enjoy it—the mutual gaze is exciting, even thrilling—and they see it as building the kind of social relationship they want with their child.

This visual aspect of caring for babies is part of our culture, and Western psychiatry endorses our conventional practice by telling us that nothing could be better for the child's mental health. The psychoanalyst Heinz Kohut, for example, proposed that the "mirroring" of mother and infant, as shown in the photo insert, is essential for the development of a child's healthy self-esteem.[17] This suggests that Gusii and Nso parents, whose culture provides them with moral and practical reasons for avoiding mutual gaze and other aspects of Western-style mother-infant interaction, are endangering their child's mental health. But speculation of this kind about the long-term development of a child may reflect a failure to consider other cultures' developmental pathways or even to imagine that there are alternatives to our way.

Findings and Reflections

Does the skin-to-skin style of infant care we found among the Gusii foster the compliance of children more than the face-to-face style characteristic of modern middle-class Americans and Europeans? Yes, concluded Heidi Keller from her comparative studies of infant development. She and her colleagues, including Relindis Yovsi, observed a sample of babies during the first three months after birth among the agrarian Nso in Cameroon and compared them with middle-class samples in Costa Rica and Greece. At eighteen months, they tested the same children on compliance tasks, asking the toddler to carry a small item. The Nso performed far better than the others, and the Costa Ricans did better than the urban Greeks. At the individual level, those children who had received more body contact in early infancy showed more compliance on the tasks.[18] The Nso mothers' interdependent infant care practices, like those of the Gusii, shape the behavior of their babies toward the compliance, respectfulness, and obedience valued in the domestic hierarchy of the agrarian family.

Interdependence Versus Independence

Our pediatrician collaborator Suzanne Dixon videotaped eighteen Gusii mothers and eighteen American mothers with their six- to twenty-five-month-old children in a maternal teaching situation.[19] Despite the fact that the task had been designed for American children, these children were visibly distressed in the situation far more frequently than the Gusii children; in addition, "the Gusii children did not resist being pulled and pushed (by their mothers), but the American infants did in almost every instance."[20] This greater compliance of Gusii children might seem anomalous to an outside observer who interprets the Gusii practices of breast-feeding on demand and mother-infant co-sleeping as "indulgence": why aren't these infants who always get their own way *more* resistant to maternal guidance than the Americans with whom they were compared? The question reveals the fallacy of interpreting Gusii practices as indulgent in the first place. They are better seen as reflecting *interdependence* as a goal of maternal care, as Keller argues.[21] The continuous provision of comfort—including tactile contact and food—seems to *prevent* the early development of a baby's willfulness rather than intensify it. The American and German mothers, with *independence* as their goal, have far less body contact with their babies, put them in separate cribs and rooms where they must comfort themselves, and engage them in distanced but contingent face-to-face interaction, and it is their babies who are more likely to resist the guidance of their mothers in an experimental situation.

Protecting their babies as well as they can from disease and injury and nurturing them throughout the first year and beyond are certainly the top priorities of Gusii mothers. But in keeping infants calm, sated, and unexcited through tactile comfort and feeding and by avoiding the face-to-face interaction that might arouse them, they are also succeeding at the goal of fostering compliance—a developmental goal critical to childhood economic performance in the domestic hierarchy of an agrarian family. Gusii mothers want—and on the whole, get—babies who accommodate to maternal wishes and give their mothers far less trouble than their American counterparts.

When we asked Gusii mothers about babies sleeping through the night, they didn't know what we were talking about—why should babies wake up? And when you look for "the terrible twos" among the Gusii, you find instead children learning to carry small objects on command and imitating their older sisters and brothers in domestic tasks. When we compare Gusii and American mothers, it is the Americans who seem to make infant care more complicated and difficult by putting their infant to sleep in their own bed in a separate room, setting the stage for sleep disruption due to infant crying.

So what are agrarian peoples, and particularly Gusii and Nso mothers, trying to foster in their infant care practices in place of the verbal skills and emotional responsiveness that middle-class

American and Europeans so keenly encourage in their babies? One answer might be that they are promoting infant health and physical growth in an environment with serious survival risks, but another is that the compliance they value is needed for adapting to the requirements of a hierarchical, food-producing family.

Is it possible that the skin-to-skin approach to infant care has other positive outcomes? The psychologist Tiffany Field has studied this question for decades.[22] Her 2010 review of the literature found that, though experimental programs for increasing touch or massage largely improve individual well-being, many basic developmental questions about touch remain unanswered. In other words, Western infant researchers have concentrated on the preferred Western style of verbal and visual interaction; studies that might show developmental advantages from skin-to-skin care have not yet been done.

∽ 5 ∽

Sharing Child Care: Mom Is Not Enough

MOTHERS RARELY RAISE their infants in isolation. Our society is exceptional in giving mothers primary responsibility for infant care in an isolated domestic setting with exceptionally sharp boundaries, with or without supplementary help from the father, a grandmother, a babysitter, or a child care center. In the world as a whole, there is greater variation in multiple-care practices: cooperation among adult women in extended or joint families; the use of children who are older siblings of the infant; the involvement of fathers; fostering and adoption, that is, sending infants to other families (related or not) for care; the hiring of live-in nannies; and the collective nurseries of Israeli kibbutz communities before 1990.

Breast-Feeding the Children of Others?

In agrarian societies, persons other than the mother are always involved in infant care. Among the Hausa, adult women in the walled compound sometimes even breast-feed each other's babies. On seeing a young Hausa woman nurse her older co-wife's baby, Sarah asked if she often did so. "Of course. This is my co-wife's week to cook for the household, so if her baby cries when she's really busy, I'll give him the breast. And the week that I cook she nurses my child when I'm really busy." Since a senior co-wife in Africa is often jealous of the "new bride," Sarah was surprised to hear of this arrangement. She learned later, however, that with a husband and four children, the older woman had decided that she needed help with domestic work and had chosen a young relative to marry her husband.

Among the Gusii, older siblings or other children routinely care for babies when the mother is working in the fields or trading in the market. A Gusii mother is horrified by the thought of another woman breast-feeding her baby, but there are other African cultures in which women breast-feed each other's infants.[1] Among the Efe pygmy hunter-gatherers of central Africa, young infants are breast-fed by most of the women in the local group; this kind of "wet-nursing" is also a common practice of the Beng of the Ivory Coast in West Africa, and it begins right after birth, when the mother has only colostrum in her breasts and she gives the baby to her own mother or another lactating kinswoman for breast-feeding.[2] Later, Beng infants are occasionally and casually breast-fed by other kin and neighbors—as well as "dry nursed" at the breasts of older women.[3] In the 1980s Sarah was told by village women in Mexico that, since formula was unaffordable, the mother-in-law of any woman who died soon after giving birth would nurse the infant. When Sarah asked how this was possible, given that the older woman was unlikely to have milk, she was told that the mother-in-law might well have a baby of her own. (The fertility rate was falling precipitously, but in the countryside families of seven and eight children were still the norm.) Even if her childbearing was over, a mother who had nursed children could do so again. All she needed to do, Sarah was assured, was have the child suck at her breast and after a while milk would come.

The anthropologists who have observed breast-feeding by women other than the child's mother often relate it to a sense of shared responsibility for children in the community. This contrasts with the historical cases from European and American history, in which rural or lower-class women were hired as wet nurses by families who could afford to pay them. It is clear that breast-feeding another woman's infant is not merely a theoretical possibility but one that has been institutionalized in some societies and reflects broader social attitudes and practices.

Trust and Sharing: Hausa Versus Gusii

The Hausa and Gusii mothers Sarah observed made strikingly different assumptions about who would help them in caring for their infants. Young Hausa mothers took it for granted that older women would share the care, whether they were in their husband's compound, where they normally resided, or visiting their mother's compound. They could make this assumption because the women of their densely populated walled compounds formed a warm, cooperative group that nurtured their children together, at least part of the time. In the context of such groups, a mother who got divorced (a frequent occurrence among the Hausa) could assume that others in her kin network would help care for her young children.

A Gusii mother, by contrast, had her own house next to her fields and for the most part could not rely on other women for help in infant care, as described in the last chapter. She assumed that her marriage was permanent (divorce, once rare, had been increasing but was still infrequent), but she was thrust into competition with the other women of the homestead over whom the husband favored among his co-wives and the future inheritance of his land. Thus, she did not *trust* the other women to have benign feelings toward her or her children. Indeed, Gusii mythology holds that cooking was invented because of jealousy between co-wives (*eng' areka*). The story goes that, in the days when Gusii ate their food raw, a woman mistakenly believed that heating food would poison her co-wife—only to discover the benefits of it! Though some co-wives and sisters-in-law got on well, women within the homestead trusted each other far less than women in the Hausa compound. A Gusii mother relied on her own older children or a child brought in from her parents' family to help her care for her infants. The sibling caregiver (*omoreri*)—usually a girl, but sometimes a boy—remained the preferred choice of all Gusii mothers, despite the complications imposed by universal schooling by the 1970s.

The sharing of infant care among women of a domestic group is found not only among the Hausa but also among the Beng of the Ivory Coast and other West African peoples. The anthropologist Alma Gottlieb emphasizes the multiplicity of caregiving for the Beng infant starting at birth. When the mother has returned to work in the fields, she has both child and adult caregivers who pass the baby around so much that by the time the mother returns later in the day she might not even know who shared the care. They engage the infant in cheerful face-to-face interactions and mock conversations in which they pretend to answer the questions they ask the baby. The spontaneous cooperation and emotional expressiveness observed by Gottlieb is in striking contrast with the infant care of the Gusii.

India and Indonesia

The sharing of infant care by mothers in a domestic setting is widespread in the joint families of India and other countries of

South Asia, where brothers and their wives and children live together as a socially integrated and hierarchical group. Daytime home observations in "Shanti Nagar," a village in Haryana state, near New Delhi in north India, conducted by the psychologist Dinesh Sharma in 1993–1994 showed that infants six to twelve months old were cared for by their mothers only about 40 percent of the time; grandmothers, aunts, and the father were among the other caregivers.[4] Care by the mother declined sharply after eighteen months, and multiple caregiving continued to be prominent during the child's second and third years after birth. In smaller households, with fewer adult women apart from the mother, fathers were more frequently involved in infant care.

The joint family is a very talkative environment. In "Shanti Nagar" thirty-five years earlier (1958–1959), when the village was more isolated and fewer mothers had attended school, "mothers and siblings talked to children constantly from birth onward," the anthropologists Ruth and Stanley Freed reported,

> and a child was always in the presence of speaking and communicating adults and children. . . . Mothers or surrogates talked to the children about what was being done. They seemed to expect them to understand even before they began to speak.
>
> Overt signs of affection . . . were directed chiefly to small children and infants. Mothers would kiss infants on the face and hug them, but would more often show affection to toddlers. . . .
>
> In most families, older children displayed affection to infants and small children.[5]

These are parents in an *agrarian* culture whose infant care practices more closely resemble those of our own culture in talk and the expression of affection than we have seen among the Gusii and Nso, but their standards of care and interaction have been developed in the context of the highly sociable setting of joint families in rural Haryana, where children as well as adults are affectionate to the young. In any event, discrete practices like talking to and kissing or hugging babies can be embedded in differing conceptions of infant care.

The anthropologist Susan Seymour reported as follows on joint families in the traditional part of the city of Bubaneshwar, capital of the northeastern Indian state of Orissa (now Odiya):

> In infancy and early childhood . . . one learns to depend upon a variety of other persons. If your mother is not free to hold and carry you, someone else will be. If you have been displaced by a new sibling, then your grandmother or aunt might become your principal source of care and attention. She might become the person who, for example, sleeps with you at night or bathes you in the morning. Although all of your basic needs will be tended to, much of the time this will be done by someone other than your mother or father. Multiple caretaking is the rule rather than the exception.[6]

Seymour presented her ethnographic material on infant care in the old section of Bubaneshwar as "socialization for interdependence," emphasizing that children were always with others, often in body contact and co-sleeping at night. At the same time, she argued that these practices did not constitute child-centered "indulgence" because the mother did not relinquish control, the prime example being the daily bath that mothers impose on their crying babies regardless of their protests. Thus, though infant care in the Indian joint family may resemble American middle-class care in the amount of talking and expressing of affection, the Indian mother's practices are distinguished by a goal of interdependence fostered by body contact and a multiplicity of caretakers and by her hierarchical insistence on practices unpleasant to the infant. As Seymour stated:

> Old Town mothers respond anywhere from several seconds to several minutes after an infant begins to cry and then rarely nurse it to satisfaction. Typically, they pick up a child and nurse it on one breast for a few minutes and then deliberately remove it before it is satisfied. When the child begins to cry again, it is given the other breast, which is again removed before the child has reached satisfaction. A complex sequence of infant crying and delayed maternal response is thus set in motion in which the mother retains control and the child has to keep "asking" for more.[7]

Is this assertion of maternal control an expression of agrarian hierarchical values in the infant care practices of the joint family? Perhaps, but if so, it shows that such values can take different forms across cultures and in India are merged or blended with other values (verbal communication, expressing affection) in forms specific to the Indian context. Beyond that context, the extended or joint families of West Africa as well as India create environments for infant care with multiple caregiving that facilitate interdependence in the developing child.

The anthropologist Birgitt Röttger-Rössler reported a similar situation among the Makassar rice farmers of south Sulawesi in Indonesia.[8] From early infancy each child is encouraged to—and does—form close relationships with numerous kin. Grandmothers are particularly prominent in infant care, and young children frequently prefer their grandmothers to their parents, even to the extent of leaving their parents. Multiple caregiving is the default condition of infancy among the Makassar, and it is also fully integrated into the life of the growing child, whose relationships with both paternal and maternal kin become crucial sources of support in adulthood.

Siblings: Children Caring for Babies

Sibling caregiving is widespread in the agrarian communities of Africa, Southeast Asia, the Pacific, and indigenous North America. But in its typical form, with a five- to nine-year-old daughter caring for a baby, it would be defined as criminal neglect in the contemporary United States, and parents who did it would be subject to arrest and a possible prison sentence. This raises the question: how is it that a practice so widespread in the agrarian world can be treated as a crime in our society? The answer begins with the difference between a rural village in which neighboring parents and other adults were available to supervise each other's children and an anonymous city in which such supervision became impossible and the exploitation of children in factories became common. Urbanization and industrialization in Europe and the United States led to the demand for laws protecting children, and with the expansion of these legal protections during the last century, responsibility for children's care was taken away from parents.

But there is more to the answer than the transformation of an agrarian society into an urban-industrial one: a six-year-old girl in an agrarian community is simply more prepared to assume responsibility for a baby than her counterpart in our contemporary society. Our children in America are raised to play, to enjoy themselves; we are less hierarchical, and we tolerate disobedience. We may be right not to trust our children with anything as serious as taking care of a baby by themselves. By comparison, the Gusii and other agrarian peoples may be taking fewer risks by strapping a baby on the girl's back for a few hours, leaving her with a few simple instructions in a place not far from adults who can be called upon if things go wrong. Their girls have learned from their earliest years that respect and obedience come first, and they have usually shown that they pay attention to parental instructions. There are still risks, ones *we* may be unwilling to tolerate, but *they* have no choice but to do so. In an African society with high fertility, there is a child labor force ready to be used. Anthropologists have also argued that sibling caregiving, involving what primatologists call a "multi-age group of juveniles," provides a better learning environment for young children than age-graded environments such as the Western school—a point we shall take up later.[9]

Fathers Caring for Infants?

Fathers are much less involved in infant care, but there is considerable variation, from extreme cases where fathers have hardly any contact with infants, as in much of East Africa (among the Gusii and other agricultural peoples), to those like the Aka hunter-gatherers of the Central African Republic, where fathers play a major part in the routine care of babies.[10] Similarly, in one of the earliest ethnographic reports, Bronislaw Malinowski described in detail the father's constant and loving care for babies among the Trobriand Islanders in Melanesia.[11] Most human societies lie between these two extremes: fathers are not responsible for day-to-day care and may or may not take an interest in their children during infancy. Fathers in India play a significant, but not primary, role in the infant care of joint families. In our field experiences, fathers in central Mexico were notable for the affection they lavished on their babies and young children. In Europe and the United States, there is a trend toward much more father involvement in infant care, even in countries that do not provide parental leave for men.

Foster Care and Adoption: Sending Babies to Others

West Africa is the region from which the proverb "It takes a village to raise a child" originated. The "village," however, is not always local but a social network of kin and others that can stretch from a remote rural area to a major city, where there are women who can be called upon to provide foster care for an infant or child. West Africa has a distinctive history of long-distance trade, apprenticeship, rural-urban migration, frequent divorce, and—in the middle decades of the twentieth century—childless women willing to take care of other women's offspring.[12] In this context, the fostering of children, young and older, near and far, became common.

Among the Mende people of Sierra Leone, there were areas where the 1975 census showed that more than half of all children under two years of age were under the care of someone other than their mother.[13] The anthropologist Caroline Bledsoe found that babies as young as four months were fostered, and in the area where she worked 40 percent of the fostered children had arrived in the community—and 23.7 percent of the out-fostered children had been sent out of it—when they were twenty-three months old or less. The usual foster parent was a "granny," sometimes but not always the child's biological grandmother; varying in age from thirty-four to elderly, she would care for the child sometimes in reciprocation for support she was receiving or sometimes because she aimed to have the child help her in the future. Infants and toddlers tended to be sent from the town to the countryside for care, while older children were sent from the countryside to the town, where they could seek educational and occupational advantages, including craft apprenticeships. For young mothers, foster care could make it easier for them to work in town or start a new marriage after divorce. For the receiving "grannies," the young children could relieve their isolation, help them in domestic tasks, and sustain their connections to the parents and others in the kin network.

As we mentioned in the introduction, fostering is common among the Hausa; indeed, almost all children are sent away for weaning, and though some are returned to their mothers after a short period, others remain with foster mothers for years. It is also common for a childless wealthy woman to adopt the child of a poor dependent, such as a house servant or her "bond-friend"— her best friend from girlhood. "Your bond-friend can deny you nothing," Sarah was told. "If you have no children of your own and she has several, you may ask her for her baby, and at weaning she will give her to you." That child will be raised to adulthood in her adoptive mother's household, marry from her house, and inherit her property. Kinship fostering in its varied forms has long been common among West African migrants to London and Paris, but we do not have observational studies of their foster care during infancy.

The Pacific

Adoption of children within the kin group is found widely across the Pacific region, including Polynesia, Melanesia, and Micronesia.[14] Some of it can be understood as redistributing children within a local kinship-based community from those who have many to those who are childless but have land or other family resources. These are small communities in which divorce and childlessness can make it convenient for a woman who has borne a child to give the child to a woman who wants a child but doesn't have one. Those who adopt children in this way have also been described as promoting social solidarity and cementing ties among kin by taking in these young children and raising them as their own. Many such adopted children know who their biological parents are. While we know of no observational studies of children adopted in infancy in Oceania, adoptive and biological babies do not seem to be treated differently.

Most of the people who receive very young children in fosterage or adoption arrangements in West Africa and the Pacific Islands are married couples or adult women of reproductive or postmenopausal ages, like the biological grandmothers of the children sent to them. In this sense there might be evolutionary requirements operating: babies are never sent for foster care or adoption to a child or adolescent, hardly ever to a single man, and rarely to unrelated strangers. Yet the high frequencies of kinship fostering among West Africans and adoption among Pacific Islanders also provide evidence that, like styles of mother-infant interaction and the sharing of care, the personnel involved in the fostering and adoption of infants is not fixed for the species, though there are limits to its variation across populations.

What Do Babies Need?
Thoughts and Reflections

What can we conclude about infant needs from the evidence provided by the varying infant care practices of diverse cultures? First of all, not all possible variations in who cares for infants are actually found in societies, suggesting limits that might really be universal. Adult women are the primary caregivers for infants, even as substitutes for the mother. The widespread role of siblings and other children as *supplementary* caregivers actually underlines this point, as the children are not given full responsibility for infants. Fathers play a variable role in infant care, often as indirect economic providers, sometimes in socially engaged supplementary care, but never as primary caregivers. These limits, of course, reflect the need for infants to be breast-fed, but in the more than 140 years since bottle-feeding was introduced in Europe and America, disengaging the mother from the necessity of feeding her baby, there have been no strong signs of a trend toward fathers (let alone children) as *primary* caregivers for infants, though fathers are playing a bigger role than before in some places. This does not mean that there could not be a society in which men are the primary infant caregivers, but it has not yet happened. Thus, there may be species-wide limits on who provides care among humans, despite the variations we have reviewed.

Second, the cultural variations in infant care practices (breast- versus bottle-feeding, skin-to-skin versus face-to-face interaction, talking or not talking to babies) can—and probably do—affect the psychological and social development of children. As we get more observations of infants in their routine settings from different parts of the world, researchers have become more proficient at distinguishing universal frames of communication like (mother-child) "reciprocal interaction" and "joint attention" from the specific learning experiences of the baby in a particular culture. The evidence increasingly shows that mothers and others provide culture-specific developmental pathways for their infants.

Third, infant care practices are clearly influenced by the social, cultural, and moral environments in which parents are embedded, but the outcomes are not simply predictable from dichotomies like agrarian versus urban-industrial societies or other conditions that seem to influence parents. Talking to babies and expressing affection to them, for example, are attributes of modern urban societies, but they are also found among agrarian peoples in West Africa and India. Beng mothers of the Ivory Coast and Hindu mothers in India and Nepal teach us that it is entirely possible to provide *both* extensive mother-infant body contact *and* face-to-face communication (although we don't know how the frequency of face-to-face behavior compares with that of Americans or Europeans). At the same time, the importance of hierarchy for agrarian parents is evident in maternal practices among the Beng, the Indians, and the Makassar, as well as the Gusii and the Nso. In the next chapter, we will consider how the lessons learned in infancy play out in the toddler period.

Finally, there are potential challenges to the assumptions of developmental psychology lurking in some of the regions we have examined. Having described the lack of face-to-face interaction and child-directed speech during infancy in East Africa, the kinship fostering of infants and toddlers in West Africa, the daily enemas for Beng infants (also found among the Zulu of South Africa), and widespread adoption in Micronesia and Tahiti, we have to ask whether the effects are as pathological as might be predicted by Western theories. If not, what do these practices tell us about the validity of those theories, taught by experts to parents as cautionary tales? Is it possible that, as Röttger-Rössler implies, the Makassar of Sulawesi and other peoples who practice multiple caregiving of infants—and who permit babies to choose their caregivers—provide their children with *more* psychological security than American and Europeans parents? If so, does that mean the psychological generalizations offered by Western psychologists unaware of these variations are not universal after all?

A young Hausa mother holds her child but looks solemnly away *(left)*. Despite this culturally enforced emotional restraint, Hausa children are still often loved and nurtured by other women, such as their mothers' co-wives *(below)*.

Both photos by Sarah LeVine, 1969.

American parents emphasize stimulating face-to-face exchange with their infants. Sarah LeVine, 2016.

A Gusii mother nurses her baby. In Kenya, skin-to-skin contact is widely viewed as more essential than face-to-face exchange. Eliza Klein, 1975.

A Gusii child with an infant on her back. In this ethnic group it is common for infants to be entrusted to the care of children as young as age six.
Sarah LeVine, 1975.

This !Kung San mother and her two young children take great pleasure in being together.
Marjorie Shostak, 1975.

Navajo mothers sometimes bind their babies to cradleboards, in sharp contrast with the physical freedom American mothers allow their infants. James Chisholm, 1975.

A Nepali mother getting her small daughter ready for the day takes pleasure in a simple ritual. Sarah LeVine, 1990.

Gusii child caretaker bathes her baby sibling, a task many American parents insist [on] *doing themselves.* Eliza Klein, 1975.

South Indian Dalit mother bathes her child in a drainage ditch, without the help of [di]stracting toys. Sarah LeVine, 2006.

Baby-sitting isn't work: a three generational Nepali family relishes simply being togeth Sarah LeVine, 1998.

Baby-sitting isn't work: In a Nepal courtyard a teenage boy and his little brother enjo *each other's company.* Sarah LeVine, 1998.

Baby-sitting isn't work: a !Kung San father plays with his baby.
Marjorie Shostak, 1975.

Baby-sitting isn't work: a Mexican grandmother takes great satisfaction in caring for her three small granddaughters.
Sarah LeVine, 1985.

Baby-sitting isn't work: a Nepali grandfather charged with his little granddaughter's care wears a joyful expression.
Sarah LeVine, 1998.

A young Yucatec Mayan girl and her mother make tortillas for dinner, a routine but complex activity such as few American preteens are expected to master. Felipe de Jesus Kumul Och, 2016.

A Nepali girl carries animal fodder down from the forest; she seems not to be bothered by the heavy load on her back. Sarah LeVine, 1990.

∞ 6 ∞

Training Toddlers:
Talking, Toileting, Tantrums, and Tasks

AMERICAN PARENTS AND grandparents find toddlers cute, lovable, amusing, endearing, even "delicious." The idea of training toddlers seems amiss: we don't *train* our toddlers—that would be coercive and domineering—we help them develop. And meanwhile we cherish them. Here are a few examples from our own experience as grandparents:

> Three-year-old Rosie says loudly, "Yesterday Monty pushed me!" The adults present, including her mother and grandparents, do not scold her for interrupting their conversation, do not correct her mistake ("yesterday" was more than a month ago), and do not point out the irrelevance of her statement to the ongoing conversation. Instead, they are charmed by her non sequitur, which they find funny and endearing. Sarah kisses her. Their reaction is typical of American and British adults to a surprising outburst from a toddler.

Sometimes a toddler's words seem to reflect her environment. For example, when Bob cuts up thirty-month-old Eva's toast for her and she says, "Good job!"—presumably echoing what her mother has said to her when she does something right. Or when twenty-nine-month-old Bella, being bathed by her grandfather, suddenly says, "I love you sooo much!"—another probable echo of maternal speech elicited by a familiar situation.

These incidents amuse us and epitomize what we love about our children and grandchildren as they become good speakers in their second and third years. But while visiting grandparents and other occasional visitors may see only cuteness, the parents have to deal with the fact that toddlers are somewhat unpredictable and capricious, they are sometimes demanding and difficult, and their tantrums are exhausting for parents. Psychologists tell us that, however we define the toddler period or early childhood— whether it's from a child's first steps to the third or even fifth birthday—the most amazing thing is how much learning and development take place in those early years. And American parents, however egalitarian, have a culturally distinctive agenda for their toddlers' development, though the shape of post-infancy parenting and child experience varies within families and communities as well as across cultures.

Canada: Inuit (Eskimo) Toddlers

Rosie's world, for example, is a far cry from that of anthropology's favorite three-year-old, Chubby Maata, a daughter of seminomadic Inuit (Eskimo) hunters on Baffin Island in the Canadian Arctic, where the anthropologist Jean Briggs observed her at home. Chubby Maata's parents love her and take good care of her, but some of their practices with children between two and four years old are startling from our point of view:

A way of stimulating children to think and value . . . was to present them with emotionally powerful problems that the children could not ignore. Often this was done by asking a question that was potentially dangerous for the child being questioned and dramatizing the consequences of various answers: "Why don't you kill your baby brother?" "Why don't you die so I can have your nice new shirt?" "Your mother's going to die—look, she's cut her finger—do you want to come live with me?" In this way, adults created or raised to consciousness, issues that the children must have seen as having grave consequences for their lives.[1]

This kind of questioning occurs frequently in the lives of Inuit toddlers as adults "playfully blow up the plots larger than life; turn them into dramas and dilemmas that children experience as dangerous," and "abandon the children—so the innocents imagine—to solve the problems with their own resources."[2] The aim, as Briggs tells us, is to introduce the child to the complexity and contradictions of life, weaving the materials most familiar to the toddler into dramas that will cause her to think.

Briggs gives us a vivid description of these patterns of adult-child play in a hunting society but does not claim to understand fully the impact of this cultural practice on the psychological development and learning of Chubby Maata and other Inuit toddlers. What are we to make of it, then, among the Inuit or anywhere else? The trouble with trying to understand toddlers is that so much is happening during those early years after infancy: they are learning a language, learning to use language, achieving control of body and emotions, forming new relationships while dependent on those formed in infancy, and learning and using skills learned from others. Even that list does not do justice to the complexity of a toddler's life.

Raising a Toddler in Peru, Nepal, or Mexico

Although developmental psychologists tend not to tackle the problem of analyzing this complexity of the toddler stage, the psychologist Barbara Rogoff did coin the term "guided participation" to represent the learning situation of the toddler in any culture.[3] The child learns to participate in the daily routines of the life around her—talking, playing, or working—as guided by adults and older children. Guided participation takes widely differing forms in different cultures. Here is an example from a Quechua-speaking agrarian community in the Peruvian Andes:

> When children are about three years old, they are allowed to do all kinds of little jobs in and around the house. Most activities are learned by observing siblings and adults. Four-year-old Victor assists the Mamani household, running errands and taking care of his two younger sisters. He brings his mother diapers, goes outside to shake small blankets, and holds the bottle for his sisters so they can drink. When about six or seven years old, he will take the animals to pasture, work on the potato fields, help to prepare meals, and select perfect *coca* leaves for offerings during fiestas.[4]

Male Caregivers for Toddlers

In the Hindu joint family of South Asia, there are many people who might guide a toddler's participation in the family's daily life. In rural Nepal, Sarah found, to her surprise, that young men took on that role. Here is an excerpt from her observations of a Hindu joint family in the farming community of Godavari outside Kathmandu[5]:

> During my first field trip, I got to know the Karkis especially well—parents, sons, daughters-in-law, and grandchildren, who lived jointly. I was passing a farmhouse with my assistant on a dazzlingly beautiful spring morning when I noticed a handsome young man with a baby in his arms pointing me out to the small boy standing beside him. A couple of days later my assistant and I noticed the young man and the children again, and this time we entered the courtyard. To my surprise I saw there were three women and two teenage girls seated on the veranda. Why, I wondered, with so many females present, were the children being cared for by a man? With my assistant translating, I learned that the women, who had been planting rice since early morning, had just come in from the fields to cook the midday meal, while the girls who had been weaving baskets and preparing vegetables were taking a rest. The young man, whose name was Arjun, explained that the girls, his younger sisters, had watched the children until, after losing his job, he'd taken their place.
>
> "It's not work," their mother, Sanu, interjected. "All he does is play."
>
> One afternoon I returned to the Karki house with my camcorder and asked if I could video Arjun and the children. A twenty-two-year-old high school graduate, Arjun had recently got married. Alone in the house (his sisters were in the fields with the other women), Arjun took his charges, his niece, Sushma, aged sixteen months, and his four-year-old nephew, Sachit, for walks around the property, had them straddle and feed leaves to a large female goat, all the while bantering with Sachit, a

hyperactive boy whom his grandmother later described to me as *badmas* (naughty). When the children's mother, Devi, crossed the yard with a load of fodder for the cattle, Sachit and Sushma ignored her, so engrossed were they with Uncle Arjun. When Sushma got sleepy, Arjun lay her down on the veranda. Covering her with a towel, he talked soothingly to her and waved flies away from her until, sure she was asleep, he turned to Sachit, opened a book, and gave the little boy a reading lesson.

Across open fields from the Karkis lived another farming family, the Bistas, who were preparing to "marry off" their oldest daughter. When, on the wedding morning, I showed up with my camera to film the proceedings, I found hired cooks preparing a feast for 300 guests and the women of the family decorating the courtyard. Meanwhile, the Bistas' son, fourteen-year-old Shiv, a snappy young fellow in a long-sleeved striped T-shirt and tight black jeans, was babysitting their toddler grandson, Ramraja. He entertained Ramraja; he fed him, changed his clothes, and, as he carried him about, had him greet the guests, palms together. Throughout the long wedding day, Shiv exuded good humor, even when, at the most solemn moment in the marriage ritual, Ramraja, who was on his shoulders, began screaming and had to be removed.

What fourteen-year-old American boy, I thought, would be willing to take care of a toddler during a five-hour wedding?

Six years later, when I returned to Godavari (with a much better grasp of the Nepali language), Shiv was off at college and Ramraja had become a lively second-grader. Meanwhile Arjun had found work in town, and his equally handsome younger brother, Prasad, had succeeded him as babysitter. Aged twenty-four, married, and an unemployed college graduate, Prasad was caring for one of Arjun's three daughters in addition to his own. Both little girls were about a year old and starting to walk. In the meantime the paterfamilias, Talik Karki, whom I hadn't met during my previous sojourn, had retired from his job in town and come home to open a teashop. From time to time Talik and Prasad would switch: Prasad would run the teashop while, with the support of his wife Sanu, Talik did what he loved to do—babysitting.

Over the two years in which I got to know these Parbatiya (Brahmin-Chetri) families in rural Godavari, I found that men of all ages took delight in small children "of the house." Whether a child was their own or their brother's, a grandchild, a boy (who would "stay" forever), or a girl (who would marry "out"), Parbatiya men would treat him or her with gentle affection, patience, and humor.

Thus, the interpersonal environments of toddlers in agrarian communities vary widely, not only in the activities involved but also in the gender of the adults who offer themselves as guides for their participation in the life of the family. The men of the Hindu joint family might represent a high point in their involvement with young children, but Sarah observed Mexican men of all ages also taking delight in young children in their families.

Another factor that varies widely is the number of adults in the household who are available to the toddler—for comfort, feeding, play, talk, and guidance that can lead to the forming of long-term relationships. Toddlers have a multiplicity of adults available for such relationships in the joint families of India and Nepal, and this is also true in West Africa and the Pacific, where fostering and adoption are also common. In some of these societies, young children are allowed to move in with kin they particularly like. By comparison, our nuclear family households seem remarkably isolated and put the burden of parenting entirely on the mother and father.

Sibling Harmony

Sarah was also impressed by the cohesion she saw in sibling groups in the villages of Nepal and south India and even more in rural Mexico, where, in the 1980s, large families were still the norm. She often heard from Mexican friends that in a fiercely competitive world they could only count on the support of close kin—and of siblings in particular. Since Sarah had seen her own children quarreling when they were young, she was curious to see how parents nurtured lifelong solidarity between siblings. To find out, she spent whole days from sunup to sundown with several Mexican families in Tilzapotla, including Rosa's. Her husband was working on the "other side" in California, leaving behind Rosa and seven children ages fifteen months to thirteen years. While the four older children went to school, the three younger ones, four-year-old Pablo, three-year-old Carlos, and the youngest, Jasmín, who had just learned to walk, were at home all day. Rosa was extremely busy, and though she herself bathed, dressed, and fed *mi reina* (my queen), as she called her little daughter Jasmín, the apple of her eye, the rest of the time the child stayed with her brothers as they played with cars and trucks in the kitchen/living room. While she went about her chores, Rosa didn't speak to the children other than to give them an occasional order. Though the boys didn't include Jasmín in their games, they were endlessly tolerant of interference. When she sat on his back as he lay on his stomach on the concrete floor, Carlos good-naturedly submitted to being "ridden." When she grabbed the car he was playing with, he let her have it and took up a different one. Switching on the boom box, Pablo began to dance to *ranchera* music to amuse his little sister, and Carlos jumped up to partner her. And so it went on all morning. When the older children came home from school and the whole family sat down to lunch, Jasmín soon became restless. After her mother set her on the floor, she went around the table bothering her siblings for a mouthful of whatever they happened to be eating. Never did any of them express irritation or refuse her.

When, after ten hours in the house, she turned off her video recorder, Sarah still hadn't seen the children squabble among themselves, much less come to blows. Throughout the day they'd been patient and kind to Jasmín, taken genuine pleasure in her antics, and played quietly together. After watching their astonishingly good-natured behavior, it occurred to Sarah that Carlos had once been the apple of his mother's eye; and before him, Pablo, and so on all the way up to thirteen-year-old María. Rosa had given the best of herself to each baby, but once a new baby arrived, her attention had to shift. From then on, the only sure way the replaced child could earn his intensely busy mother's approval was by being gentle with the baby who now filled his slot. To become a full member of the family "team," he had to learn patience and kindness and to find delight in his "follower." On this particular day, Rosa was always within earshot; however, had Sarah been in the house on a Saturday when Rosa went to town, she would have seen the "team" functioning just as smoothly under the supervision of María, the eldest daughter. She would have heard the thirteen-year-old give the occasional order and seen the younger children obey; the rest of the time they would have spent playing.

Thus, the agrarian world contains examples of toddler environments that promote sibling solidarity and emotional relationships with multiple adults—including men—as well as those that inhibit the display of affection and foster responsibility in tasks. American parents cannot simply borrow wholesale practices predicated on large households with hierarchical values, but we might be able to learn from them—for example, that parents can be affectionate without giving up on responsibility training. But

first we need to take a closer look at specific problems and opportunities for parents in early childhood: language acquisition,
toilet training, temper tantrums, and learning to become responsible—all of which vary widely across cultures.

Talking

American parents care a great deal about talking and hope to
see their children talking as early as possible. In Chapter 3, we
saw the contrast between American parents' practice of talking to
their babies—conducting "play dialogues," "mock conversations,"
or "protoconversations" in which they ask questions of the infant
and provide the infant's answers—and the views of East African
mothers we've worked with, who think talking to babies is silly.
The African mothers have noticed that children acquire the abilities to speak and understand speech *without* direct instruction
during the second and third years of life; this finding from folk
knowledge is confirmed by linguists who studied language acquisition in remote corners of the world during the second half of
the twentieth century. There have been no reports of populations
in which a significant proportion of children—or any children at
all—grow up unable to speak because their parents neglected to
train them in the local language. In other words, the acquisition
of the basic grammatical competence to make and understand
sentences in a particular language during the early years (especially between eighteen and thirty-six months) is a robust universal development in humans that makes few demands on parents,
particularly if the family's residence offers an environment full
of opportunities for watching and participating in speech every
day—even when most of it is not directed to the child. Agrarian
societies, including those of eastern Africa with their mother-
child households, also offer such opportunities: older siblings,

cousins, adult women, and, at least occasionally, men talk inside and outside the house daily. The youngest child is surrounded by a flow of verbal interaction in and around the home.

But what about the sharply bounded, often isolated households found in modern urban societies, where a firstborn two-year-old may be alone with his mother most of the day? These might seem from the viewpoint of an agrarian society to put the child at risk of speech deprivation. In fact, however, the toddler has a modern mother who comes culturally equipped with the desire to talk to and with him (as she did when he was a baby) and deluges him with a flow of child-directed speech that guarantees the child will acquire the abilities to speak and comprehend the local language. Yes, it's true that if an American mother did *not* speak to her firstborn toddler, hire a babysitter, or put him in day care, the child's language development could be delayed, but such a woman would be considered so inadequate, and possibly mentally ill, that she might be legally declared an "unfit mother." We tend to be so confident that mothers want to talk to their children that we perceive no risk in a housing standard that puts mothers into isolation with their toddlers. In fact, from an American point of view, it is the rural African mothers, with their infrequent face-to-face verbal interaction during infancy and after, who put their children at risk of failing, not to acquire the language of their community, but to build the vocabulary that will help them in school.

Children learn to talk without any special effort by parents or others, but a child's culture-specific language skills and vocabulary can reflect, and be amplified by, parental priorities and training, a process called "language socialization."[6] Parents everywhere, though they may not know about vocabulary inputs and outputs, are aware that it's not enough for a growing child to be able to make and understand sentences; the child must also *use* the language according to local standards and know what kinds of things to talk about. In all the places Sarah has worked, greeting correctly is considered most important and mothers begin teaching babies how to do this from a very early age. At six months, South Asian babies are taught to place their palms together and bow their heads. A small child learns to say "Namaste" well before even the best brought up American or British child utters a greeting. But it may not be important to master other kinds of verbal exchange until much later, as the anthropologist-psychologist team Sara Harkness and Charles Super discovered.[7]

Kenya: Obeying Without Speaking

When working among the Kipsigis people in Kenya (just east of the Gusii), Harkness and Super launched a study that required three-year-old children to answer questions. In the study, a local woman known to the children asked them questions in a familiar setting, but only 10 percent of the children answered. The children were well acquainted with the researchers and had been observed talking among themselves and engaging in "boisterous" play, yet when asked to do a test that required talking to an adult, they would not comply. By contrast, on a test that required only pointing to the right answer, most of them did it without hesitation. Harkness and Super observed that in routine interactions with their mothers the Kipsigis children followed her commands while saying nothing in return. In other words, they acquired conventions of language use in a child-adult situation that led them to obey instructions *without* speaking; to do otherwise would be disrespectful. Harkness and Super identify these conventions as first steps in the Kipsigis child's learning both obedience and respect, which are required by the hierarchy of the agrarian family.

Thus, children begin learning the local conventions of language use during the second year of life and can be observed using them in speech situations by the time they are three. By that age, their communications have already been shaped by practices reflecting their mother's goals.

So mothers in agrarian societies, concerned that their toddlers avoid being disrespectful, train them in the conventions of respectful greetings to strange adults. People like the Beng of the Ivory Coast, however, go far beyond the teaching of a formal greeting to familiarize their babies with a variety of other people almost from birth, so that they will be spontaneously friendly to strangers and engage in greetings they have heard others use.

Direct Instruction Among Chinese

English-speaking Canadian mothers in Vancouver, like their counterparts south of the border, provide their toddlers with what has been called "conversational apprenticeship," a form eschewed by Chinese immigrant mothers in the same city. The language researchers Judith Johnston and Anita Wong found that

> the Chinese mothers were much less likely to report that they often prompt their young child for personal narratives, talk with the child about nonshared events of the day, or allow the child to converse with adults who are not family members. Such activities would treat the child as a potentially equal conversational partner and hence reflect an expectation for independence and early verbal competence. . . . These are not the childrearing goals of Chinese parents, who instead value social interdependence and hold only modest performance expectations for preschoolers.[8]

The Chinese immigrant mothers did not believe in treating their two-year-olds as equal conversational partners. They saw their young children as apprentices in an age-graded respect hierarchy that accorded with Confucian ideology. This basically agrarian model—retained among Chinese immigrants to Taipei, Hong Kong, Vancouver, and Los Angeles—has ancient origins in concepts like *guan*, which means "governing" but also "caring for," and *chiao shun*, which means "training," but "with parental concern." The Chinese concepts combine parental authority with love: loving your child, you want to train him properly for a future educational career, and the child must accept the parent's instructions. This starts early, with mothers engaging in a form of didactic guidance that seems domineering to a contemporary American parent. In the introduction, we mentioned Heidi Fung's observations of Taipei mothers "haranguing" their three-year-olds about moral transgressions, but this style is also evident in didactic routines designed to train the young children for school performance, including the use of flash cards. To some extent, the Chinese mothers seem like "old-fashioned" American mothers of the 1930s, but they are drawing on ancient Chinese traditions that honor academic training, with a calculating eye for what might foster it in a new environment.

In mainland China, there are signs of change, from "direct instruction to child-initiated activities" in preschools, as represented by the Ministry of Education's 2001 *Guidelines for Kindergarten,* which is said to reflect European influences.[9] The director of a Beijing preschool studied in 1985 and 2003 by educational researchers Joseph Tobin and Yeh Hsueh reported that "storytelling is a time-honored preschool activity. In the past, teachers told or read stories and the children just listened. When we decided to change this to let the children be the story-tellers, we struggled with how to get the children to listen. . . . Eventually, the children . . . asked the questions of each other."[10]

Yet there are dissident voices. Here is Professor Li of Yunnan Normal University in Kunming:

I don't think the new guidelines represent our future. The *Guidelines* are too westernized. Westernized education prioritizes individuality, democracy and equality. This educational ideal is in direct conflict with our Confucian culture. A tree transplanted from the West into Confucian soil will have difficulty taking root. The Confucian tradition fits with Chinese parents' experiences growing up and with their wishes for their children's education. . . . Among ordinary people there is a widespread desire to restore the traditional education approach, that is, to restore Confucian culture.[11]

Tobin and his colleagues suggest that in contemporary China "a play-oriented, child-centered approach is dominant, a didactic . . . approach is residual; and a hybrid form, combining the two, is emerging."[12] But they also suggest that the ideological trends in preschool education may be more chaotic and unpredictable than any such clear-cut formulation implies. In fact, the "Confucian soil" of the People's Republic of China had been disturbed before, notably by Mao Zedong during the Cultural Revolution of the 1960s and 1970s, in which Confucius was demonized and latter-day "Confucians" condemned. Meanwhile, neo-Confucianism thrived in Taiwan and other places in the Chinese diaspora. There may be a parallel between our modern turn against the agrarian values embodied in Judeo-Christian traditions and China's more recent struggles with the agrarian values embodied in Confucianism; freeing the individual from submission to authority is a theme of both. One location for this struggle is the environment in which children first learn to communicate with adults. But recent comparisons by Peggy Miller and her colleagues show American mothers of toddlers to be more child-centered and egalitarian than their didactic and authoritative Chinese counterparts—so far.[13]

Even though agrarian cultures are similar in their more or less traditional standards of unilateral communication with toddlers, they are far from uniform. The East African (Gusii, Kipsigis) mother issues commands: I talk, you do what I say (and don't reply verbally). The Chinese mother commands a toddler's attention: I talk, you listen (for your own moral benefit). The East African communication takes place in a context of labor-intensive agriculture carried out by women and children. The Chinese communication takes place in a context defined by moral virtue, learning, and filial piety—as conceptualized in ancient (Confucian) texts. So as Chinese toddlers learn to communicate, they acquire moral messages from their mothers as standards for their own behavior.

Coded Formulas for Speaking and Feeling

These conventions of language—greetings, US and Canadian conversational apprenticeship, Chinese didactic narratives, East African commands—are just a few examples of the many coded formulas that toddlers acquire as they learn to speak a given language. They demonstrate that, when children learn to speak, they acquire culture-specific templates for communication that carry emotional and moral meanings.

Children learn the emotions involved in culture-specific relationships through language. The anthropologist Bambi Schieffelin has described how, among the Kaluli people of Papua New Guinea, little boys learn to use the unique kin term *adɛ,* which can be translated as "pity," to ask their older sisters to help them, and how mothers foster a caring attitude in the older sisters by using that term.[14] In Japan, the linguist Patricia Clancy shows, mothers use the word *kowai* ("scary/be afraid of") to teach their young children not to play with matches or fire and not to use the word for harmless insects, in part through modeling fear (of matches but not insects) in their own facial expressions and tone of voice.[15] These terms become not only parts of the children's language but also parts of their behavioral repertoire and psychological makeup.

The United States: The "Problem" of Toilet Training

Contemporary American mothers may say it's up to the child when he or she will be toilet-trained, but they generally expect it by three years of age, sometimes earlier. Despite the ease provided by modern disposable diapers, toilet training remains an aspect of the toddler period that gives mothers some anxiety. This has partly to do with our concern about cleanliness—it isn't that long ago that "cleanliness is next to godliness" was repeated without irony. This anxiety also has partly to do with Freud's concept of an "anal stage" of development as a unique source of parent-child conflict that generates emotional problems like obsessive-compulsive disorder—an idea that has survived with little empirical support for roughly a century. (Freud formulated it in 1905; we're not certain when its influence expired—or if it has.)

Some American and British mothers (and nannies) of the 1930s and 1940s claimed that they toilet-trained their children during the first year of life, citing the lack of washing machines for cloth diapers as a reason (retrospectively). Half of the mothers in the Boston area study of the early 1950s (mentioned in Chapter 2) started to toilet-train their babies at or before nine months of age; 60 percent of the whole sample had completed training by nineteen months.[16] The Newsons report that, in 1959–1960, 83 percent of their mothers in Nottingham, England, started toilet training before twelve months, but 40 percent "did not expect to finish with daytime nappies [diapers] until after the child was two years old."[17] However, they provide evidence from other British studies that casts doubt on retrospective maternal reports on this subject. (Their doubts were strongly confirmed by subsequent studies that discredited the maternal interview as a source of valid evidence on child rearing.[18]) What is interesting about those mid-twentieth-century studies is that so many mothers tried to claim earlier toilet training as a badge of honor for themselves and their offspring; it's also interesting, in retrospect, that the researchers on both sides of the Atlantic took toilet training so seriously as an aspect of parenting in their publications.

Although good survey data are not available, it seems clear that toilet training during the first eighteen months was common in the period 1930–1960, with the age rising thereafter to twenty-four to thirty-six months by the 1980s. Factors responsible for this trend include the greater availability of washing machines (and, later, disposable diapers) and the advice of pediatric experts like T. Berry Brazelton, who as early as 1962 advocated a "child-oriented approach" in which the child decides when she is ready, at no earlier than eighteen months of age.[19]

China and India

So it is possible to toilet-train infants and young toddlers; our recent ancestors did so. This would come as no surprise to parents in China and India, where the toilet training of very young children is routine.[20] Mothers or grandmothers use sounds like hissing to create an association between the sound and the urination or bowel movement, so that they can later use the sound to get the child to excrete on demand. These agrarian folk discovered the learning mechanism of associative conditioning for which I. P. Pavlov, working with dogs, won the Nobel Prize in 1906. Translating folk science into practice, Chinese parents put split-crotch pants on toddlers to prevent accidents from soiling their clothes, and they have uncarpeted floors that can be easily cleaned. As for India, the anthropologists Ruth and Stanley Freed report the following from the village outside of New Delhi:

> Socialization for handling bodily wastes was begun by the end of the first month after birth. Mothers with a number of children might start sooner. When a child was about a month old, its mother periodically dangled the baby between her knees. She held the infant in an upright walking position under its arms and said "Se, Se" repeatedly to have the child urinate. This act, a form of conditioning, was performed at least every two hours or whenever the child seemed restless or uncomfortable. Training was initially for urination, but later the same procedure was used for defecation. The shirt, the only garment an infant wore, was very practical for purposes of elimination. . . .
>
> Any woman who carried an infant around was periodically seen to hold it between her knees. As a woman held the infant and said, "Se Se," she also shook it a bit so that, as mothers said, "The Child will understand" what was wanted. . . .
>
> . . . An infant cannot control its limbs well enough to squat until it is about one-and-a-half years of age. Then a mother would put the child in the squat position to defecate. By the time a child was two years old, most mothers in Shanti Nagar claim that the child knew what to do and that there no longer was a need to worry about the formation of this habit. A mother also taught the child how to clean itself with water using the left hand; an older sister might take over this function from the mother. Most mothers said that by the time a child was two to two-and-a-half years old the child could and did clean itself. A few mothers indicated that some children took until the age of three.[21]

Perhaps most interesting in this account is that the training starts right after birth but is not completed until twenty-four to thirty months of age or even later, although in the Indian case "completion" means cleaning oneself with water after defecation using only the left hand. Seymour's report from Bubaneshwar in Orissa is similar:

> One is allowed to grow up at one's own pace. . . . Old Town infants are not diapered. Whoever is holding or carrying an infant tries to sense when it is about to urinate or defecate and hold it away from her or his clothing so that it can eliminate directly onto the earthen or the cement courtyard floor, which can be easily washed. Accidental wetting of clothing is taken in stride. As a child develops its crawling and walking skills, it is encouraged to eliminate in a corner of the courtyard or into the open drains in front of the house.[22]

One might say that Brazelton's child-oriented toilet training was invented in India, although the context is quite different: Indian mothers' concern about cleanliness is grounded in a religious conception of purity and pollution that leads to bathing babies daily. Furthermore, Indian houses of the past, particularly in villages, did not have toilets or latrines; adults went to "the jungle"—that is, nearby fields and pastures—to defecate. Each child eventually learned to do that, but in the meantime their accidents were treated casually. The Indians could be seen from a Western perspective as both obsessed with purity and pollution and all too nonchalant about training. From an Indian perspective, however, there are fairly clear age-graded expectations for the child to acquire certain skills, combined with an elastic attitude toward individual differences among toddlers. Most noteworthy is the apparent lack of anxiety about toilet training among

Indian mothers. They know what to do and have a realistic understanding that it will work—eventually if not immediately. This is, of course, the attitude of an experienced mother, and there is no shortage of experienced mothers ready to act as authoritative guides in an Indian joint family.

Africa, the Pacific, and South America

In the rest of the agrarian world—from Africa to the Pacific and South America—there is no instance we know of in which mothers are anxious about toilet training or would even consider it an urgent priority for their toddlers' development. They are more likely to assume that it will happen and that, before its completion, they will deal with accidents, without diapers, using materials at hand. Many of these mothers are living in tropical places where much time is spent in outdoor settings where the excreta of small children and domestic animals can be simply swept out of sight and is later naturally degraded. If they are without anxiety, it is because they are unaware of the risks associated with toilet training, whether those posited by Freud's concept of the anal stage of psychosexual development or the health risks in living without modern sewage disposal and clean water. For example, as mentioned earlier, the Gusii in the 1950s depended on water brought up by young girls from streams flowing between the hills on which they lived. Like Indian villagers, the Gusii were without latrines and used pastures instead. The torrential rains each year would wash feces down the pastures into the streams, and there would be an epidemic of typhoid, a diarrheal disease that killed children and some adults. Then wells were dug that provided clean water and prevented the epidemics; latrines would come later. When we conducted our study of infants, the Gusii were still in transition to a more sanitary lifestyle with its health benefits, but the toilet training of young children was little affected and was not a source of anxiety for mothers or others.

If humans can be trained in toileting in the first year of life or shortly thereafter, what does that mean about contemporary American practice? Our practices are grounded not only in the ultraconvenience of the modern disposable diaper but also in the prescription that a toddler must voluntarily choose the timing of this developmental step rather than have the mother impose it. Cultural preference and technology trump nature again, for toilet training as for breast-feeding, but as with feeding practices, toilet training remains a source of anxiety for American mothers. It may be that the anxiety interferes with the mother's confidence that she can ever train the child, resulting in endless postponement.

Tantrums

What do we know about tantrums? Are they something universal and necessary in human emotional development or just something American toddlers do to harass their already harried parents? Tantrums have only rarely been studied by child psychologists or, so far as we can tell, anyone else. Wherever she worked, mothers assured Sarah that some young children had something like tantrums, yet for all the time she spent observing children at home, she very rarely saw one. When Fred, a boy who was the largest and most physically active child in our Gusii infant study, was just over two, Sarah saw him throw himself to the ground kicking and screaming. But she never saw another Gusii child have a tantrum.

American Tantrums

A major study of tantrums in American children was conducted through parental reports on 355 children ages eighteen to sixty

months at the University of Wisconsin in 2000.[23] The two articles reporting on this study make for therapeutic reading: if
your child's tantrums aren't as bad or as frequent as those described in the articles, you may feel relieved. For example, the
researchers report that "up to 3 or 4 years, many children have a
tantrum on the average of once per day." Three-quarters of the
tantrums lasted five minutes or less (which means that one out
of four lasted more than five minutes—close to eternity for a parent!) Tantrums were most frequent when the child was thirty to
thirty-six months old and then decreased almost by half by forty-
two to forty-six months of age. This resembles the age distribu-
tion found in one of the earlier Berkeley longitudinal studies, so
it may represent a more general pattern for Americans.[24]

English Tantrums

In their interview study of mothers of four-year-olds in Nottingham, England, in the middle 1960s, the Newsons found that 36
percent of the children had a tantrum at least once a week.[25] Fo-
cusing on social class differences, they found that almost half of
the children in the lowest of five social classes had a tantrum that
frequently, whereas only one-quarter of those in the highest two
classes did. However, that lowest class was distinguished by the
parents' teasing of toddlers to elicit a tantrum, which they found
amusing; this practice was absent among all the other parents,
whose children had tantrums much less frequently. One-third of
the Nottingham parents as a whole, but only 20 percent of the
highest two classes, "smacked" their children for tantrums. The
Newsons interpret the lower frequency of tantrums in the highest social classes as due to educated parents using verbal reasoning to prevent tantrums—a theory that strikes us as more likely
to reflect what experts thought in the mid-twentieth century than
the reality of child development. But their account also reflects

working-class affection for children. Here is a description by a miner's wife of her daughter's tantrums:

> Not very often—but when it comes it's a smasher! It's a wonder that the door's never come off its hinges. She bangs it, and she stamps, and she has them chairs over. Then the rug comes up— *that* goes through it, *that* gets kicked to bits.
>
> I leave her alone, I just leave her alone. She finishes, and then I'll say "Oh, what's the matter, me old flower, then?"—and she'll come and maybe sit on my knee, or she'll lean here, and I'll just stroke her head and talk to her. She's all right then.[26]

Peru: The Matsigenka

Do tantrums occur in other cultures? The anthropologist Allen Johnson, in his book on the Matsigenka—an isolated people who combine foraging with agriculture in the Peruvian Amazon—has a section titled "Temper Tantrum as Key Transition." Describing children during the second and third years as having "a strong sense of entitlement" and not complying readily with their mothers' commands, Johnson relates the child's anger to the mother's weaning him from the breast because she is pregnant:

> At this point Matsigenka children enter a temper-tantrum phase consisting of lengthy protests many times a day for periods of up to several months. Angry, especially at the mother, for weaning and for not picking her up, the child rushes at her, threatens to hit her, picks up twigs and dirt and throws them at her, falls to the ground screaming, refuses to budge, engages in long dramatic wailing, and in general uses the limited means at her disposal to show her rage and hurt the offending mother.

Small issues that previously would have been resolved quickly, like being refused an item of clothing or a toy, now seed storms of protest. Mostly harmless, the tantrum child can occasionally cause great damage, as when Apa (forty-four months old) "accidentally" set fire to his house while his father was working in his garden: the house and all possessions in it burned to ashes, a devastating loss. This incident happened a few months after his baby sister was born.[27]

Johnson also describes a case in which a "boy had been throwing tantrums of several hours' duration each day for six months and showed no sign of abandoning the effort." He calls the temper tantrum phase "a defining moment in Matsigenka child development, a fundamental separation when children learn with finality that they no longer command their caretakers, that they can no longer intimidate and manipulate with tears. . . . Between tantrum episodes, the child seems perfectly normal, playing, helping around the house, participating in meals."[28]

When the tantrum phase is over, children are reported to be more self-reliant, calm, and responsible. The Matsigenka toddlers "firmly demand what they want." They are described, like American toddlers, as children who are not used to being denied their wishes—unlike their age-mates in many other agrarian societies.[29] In a more recent account by Carolina Izquierdo, however, the youngest children do imitate their parents in productive tasks, often voluntarily, occasionally when directed by the mother. By six or seven, "boys start accompanying fathers to hunt, fish and plant in the gardens, while the girls remain close to their mothers to observe and help with cooking, sweeping, weaving, washing clothes, child care, and women's work in the gardens."[30] In other words, Matsigenka children's participation in productive work resembles that of children in other agrarian societies, though their parents' deliberate training may begin somewhat later, after earlier periods of entitlement and tantrums.

The Pacific

This hunch is confirmed by another recorded case of tantrums from the Micronesian islands of Palau in the Pacific. The anthropologist Homer Barnett reports:

> Five-year-old Azu trails after his mother as she walks along the village path, whimpering and tugging at her skirt. He wants to be carried, and he tells her so, loudly and demandingly, "Stop! Stop! Hold me!" His mother shows no sign of attention. She continues her steady barefooted stride, her arms swinging freely at her sides, her heavy hips rolling to smooth the job of her walk and steady the basket of wet clothes she carries on her head. She has been to the washing pool and her burden keeps her neck stiff, but this is not why she looks impassively ahead and pretends not to notice her son. Often before she has carried him on her back and an even heavier load on her head. But today she has resolved not to submit to his plea, for it is time for him to begin to grow up.
>
> Azu is not aware that the decision has been made. Understandably, he supposes that his mother is just cross, as she often has been in the past, and that his cries will soon take effect. He persists in his demand, but falls behind as his mother firmly marches on. He runs to catch up and angrily yanks at her hand. She shakes him off without speaking to him or looking at him. Enraged, he drops solidly on the ground and begins to scream. He gives a startled look when this produces no response, then rolls over on his stomach and begins to writhe, sob, and yell. He

beats the earth with his fists and kicks it with his toes. This hurts and makes him furious, the more so since it has not caused his mother to notice him. He scrambles to his feet and scampers after her, his nose running, tears coursing through the dirt on his cheeks. When almost on her heel he yells and, getting no response, drops to the ground.

By this time his frustration is complete. In a rage he grovels in the red dirt, digging his toes into it, throwing it around him and on himself. He smears it on his face, grinding it in with his clenched fists. He squirms on his side, his feet turning his body through an arc on the pivot of one shoulder.

A man and his wife are approaching. . . . The couple pass Azu sprawled on the path a few yards behind his mother. They have to step around his frenzied body, but no other recognition is taken of him, no word is spoken to him or to each other. There is no need to comment. *His tantrum is not an unusual sight, especially among boys of his age or a little older* [emphasis added]. There is nothing to say to him or about him. . . .

Two girls, a little older than Azu, stop their play to investigate. . . . The girls stand some distance away, observing Azu's gyrations with solemn eyes. Then they turn and go back to their doorway, where they stand, still watching him but saying nothing. Azu is left alone, but it takes several minutes for him to realize that this is the way it is to be. Gradually his fit subsides and he lies sprawled and whimpering on the path.

Finally he pushes himself to his feet and starts home, still sobbing and wiping his eyes with his fists. As he trudges into the yard he can hear his mother shouting at his sister, telling her not to step over the baby. Another sister is sweeping the earth beneath the floor of the house. . . . Glancing up, she calls shrilly to Azu, asking him where he has been. He does not reply, but

climbs the two steps to the threshold of the doorway and makes
his way to a mat in the corner of the house. There he lies quietly
until he falls asleep.

   This has been Azu's first painful lesson in growing up. . . .
Soon or late the child must learn not to expect the solicitude,
the indulgence and the warm attachment of earlier years.[31]

Barnett makes it clear that this is a real transition in parental
treatment of the Palau child, as

watchful guidance and tenderness is suddenly replaced by parental detachment and querulous impatience, particularly on
the part of mothers. Instead of gradually relaxing their concern
for children, they rather abruptly turn away from them and make
them take care of themselves; instead of carrying them everywhere, they make them walk, instead of answering to their cry,
they go about their business and ignore the child's vigorous protests. At about this time, too, they begin to shout at their children and attempt to apply the ineffective disciplinary device of
speaking harshly to them. Chiding replaces indulgence.[32]

Girls are said to have a more gradual and easier transition than
boys, since they are kept on a "tighter rein" to begin with. "But the
end is the same: a . . . pre-adolescent whose fathers and mothers
are people to whom respect, obedience and labor are due."[33] The
agrarian pattern, then, is present in Palau but delayed until five or
six years of age; that delay seems to create a turbulent transition,
especially for boys.

   By delaying demands for obedience early in the toddler period,
agrarian parents who use the labor of older children in domestic
production may be setting the stage for a transition character-
ized by tantrums. Anthropologists' accounts of childhood from

Indonesia—by Harald Broch from the island of Bonerate near Sulawesi (Celebes) in Indonesia and by Doug Hollan and Jane Wellenkamp—generally support this idea.[34]

Tantrums are found widely among populations but are not universal culturally or individually, and they are largely confined to a particular period, between two and five years of age. Parents may be able to avoid their occurrence by the kind of training in early compliance found in the African societies we have observed, while they seem more likely to occur where parents play with their younger toddlers, creating expectations incompatible with the demands of domestic work. Are tantrums more frequent or intense in America than elsewhere? Developmental psychologists could help American parents by doing the research to answer this question.

Tasks

In many agrarian societies, as African and some Latin American observations show, parents tend to see eighteen-month-old toddlers as little workers to be initiated into a role in the domestic production team by being trained in tasks like taking small items from one adult to another on command. A few years later, when they are five or six years old, parents will assign them real responsibilities like taking care of a baby, often carried on the back, or herding sheep and goats while the older boys are herding cattle. That's what we observed among the Gusii in the 1950s, and the pattern was similar in much of the agrarian world. Tasks assigned to young children among the Kpelle of Liberia, the Maya of Yucatán, and the Quechua of the Peruvian Andes resemble those of the Gusii of Kenya. The same could be said for Polynesia, as documented in the accounts of the anthropologists Mary Martini and John Kirkpatrick for the Marquesan Islands and in Raymond

Firth's classic ethnography of the Tikopia, based on fieldwork conducted in 1928–1929.[35]

Samoa

All of these Polynesian patterns seem in evidence in Samoa, where many anthropologists have worked, including Margaret Mead, Elinor Ochs, and Jeanette Mageo.[36] Young children are pressed into service at many tasks and help out in the home. Mageo, who lived there for many years, reported that "children were, and indeed are, the household work force." Yet she observed their ambivalence in the course of child development:

> What helps young people move past the rage displayed in separation tantrums, and in jumping-mouth insolence, then partially disguised in resentful service is that, from childhood onward, *tautua* not only means subordination to elders but also command of subordinates. Thus, children may be saddled with sibling care but also have full authority to demand attention and compliance from younger ones and to beat them should they demur, which affords considerable opportunity to disguise and displace rage.[37]

Mageo's approach goes beyond observing children working in Samoa to looking at their emotional relationships with parents and other adults in the course of psychological development. But the developmental pattern she identifies is culturally rooted in Samoan social life and seems unlike that of agrarian societies of Africa.

The Pacific: Melanesia

There seem to be exceptions to the agrarian pattern in Melanesia. There one can find examples of young children who, like the aforementioned toddlers of Bonerate and Toraja, spend their days free not only of productive work but also of adult supervision and who occasionally defy their parents and even slap them! The first observers who reported this were anthropological pioneers Bronislaw Malinowski and Margaret Mead. Malinowski noted that "children in the Trobriand Islands enjoy considerable freedom and independence. . . . A simple command, implying the expectation of natural obedience, is never heard from parent to child in the Trobriands. People will sometimes grow angry with their children and beat them in an outburst of rage; but I have quite as often seen a child rush furiously at his parent and strike him."[38] And Mead, who spent six months among the Manus (population: 2,000) in the Admiralty Islands near New Guinea in 1928, saw that

> the parents who were so firm in teaching the children their first steps become wax in the young rebels' hands when it comes to any matter of social discipline. They eat when they like, play when they like, sleep when they see fit. They use no respect language to their parents. . . . The veriest urchin can shout defiance and contempt at the oldest man in the village. . . . They do no work. Girls, after they are eleven or twelve, perform some household tasks, boys hardly any until they are married. . . .
>
> The children are perfectly trained to take care of themselves; any sense of physical insufficiency is guarded against. They are given their own canoes, paddles, swings, bows and arrows.[39]

In Mead's account, Manus children acquire in their play groups the skills in subsistence and food-processing that they will use as adults through their imitation of older children. But they do not contribute to domestic economic production during childhood.

This seems to defy the imperative of child labor we have attributed to agrarian peoples.

On the other hand, Karen Ann Watson-Gegeo, who more recently conducted a ten-year study of child-rearing among the Kwara'ae people of Malaita in the Solomon Islands (like Mead's Admiralty Islands, part of Melanesia), presents the following picture:

> As in many Pacific island environments, the Kwara'ae push their children to be adult as soon as possible. Kwara'ae children participate in agriculture and household work from three years of age. . . . At three . . . girls are given their first machetes (usually downsized adult machetes) and begin working in the family gardens. They also begin caring for their younger sibling with adult supervision and by age six or seven may take care of infants without adult supervision for several hours at a time. . . . Three-year-old girls also carry heavy loads of firewood on their backs from the forest, build cooking fires, wash clothes and dishes (including glass and pottery), peel potatoes, carry water from streams, sweep floors and neatly cut the grass in the yards around the houses. From age five girls and often boys make gardens of their own, planting, harvesting, and selling the produce in the market or contributing it to family meals. Five-year-old boys build their own small houses. At five or six years children are given piglets of their own to raise. An 11-year-old girl can run a household and a set of gardens entirely by herself.[40]

Thus Kwara'ae parents put their children to work as toddlers, resembling parents in Africa and Mexico more than the Manus in another part of Melanesia. But the Manus rely heavily on fishing, conducted by teams of adult men, rather than domestic agriculture.

Summary and Conclusions

Children from one to five years of age go through an astounding amount of physical and psychological growth. We can track bodily growth through height and weight, language acquisition through mastery of a language (or two), cognitive development through the mastery of concepts, and emotional maturity in the child's increasing control according to cultural standards. The best way to describe this development is "guided participation," in which the little boy or girl is actively learning in a social environment, guided by parents and others. Toddlers are visibly persons-in-the-making, manifesting some tendencies they will have the rest of their lives while also experiencing transitions marked by tantrums or toilet training that are no more than temporary. By the time they are five years old, toilet training and tantrums may be in the distant past, and they have gained control of their bodies and emotions.

In some cultures, parents think early childhood is best devoted to play; in others, parents stigmatize play as a diversion from the work toddlers should do. Some of this variation is due to the difference between the agrarian societies, in which labor-intensive food production requires that young children learn to work at the bottom of a family hierarchy, and post-agrarian societies, like our own, in which child labor is forbidden and parents favor play and other activities. But in some cultures in Oceania—the largely agrarian Pacific region—toddlers roughly two to five years old enjoy a period of play that is strikingly different from what we have seen in Africa and Mesoamerica. Margaret Mead described children who were essentially left to their own devices and did not work until six years old or later. These observations led us to wonder whether the toddler's expectations of parental attention, affection, and tolerance in these Pacific contexts (and here in America) make temper tantrums more likely.

The parenting of children during the first five years has many strands distinctive to that period, and we have touched on only a few: the acquisition of cultural meanings with first language development, toilet training, temper tantrums, and task assignments. We tend to believe that, as found in Heidi Keller's comparative study cited earlier, the treatment of babies in a particular culture prepares them for their lives as toddlers, and conversely, that the child's guided participation after infancy is affected by earlier treatment as a baby. We return to questions of continuity and discontinuity in Chapter 8, where we consider the evidence on precocious children and parental influence. In the next chapter, we take a look at the parenting of older, "school-age" children, roughly five to ten years old, as it varies across cultures, particularly those without schooling.

∽ 7 ∾

Childhood:
School, Responsibility, and Control

FOR AMERICAN CHILDREN and their parents, the first days
of school, or preschool, are a major transition from the world
of home to that of the school. But in agrarian societies without
schools, children stay at home and continue to contribute to the
household economy with greater proficiency and more responsibility as time goes on. In their quest for universals, psychologists
once proposed the five- to seven-year-old period as a moment
of developmental transition for all humans (and for theories of
psychological development), and it does seem that parents everywhere consider their children after this period to be more capable
of responsibility than before it.[1] But the cultures of the world
present so many exceptions that this is no more than a vague
approximation. The emerging capabilities of children cannot be
read from a preordained timetable for the species.

In agrarian settings, this ambiguity has to do with the apprenticeship pattern: a child who has observed a task being performed

by others in the home starts doing it and then, either gradually or suddenly, assumes responsibility for it.[2] The age of task performance may also vary across siblings in a family and across families within a community. But there is no doubt that parenting changes in "later childhood"—the years from ages five to ten—as the child matures physically, intellectually, and emotionally.

In this chapter, we continue to examine how parents provide cultural pathways for their children's development. All parents want similar things *for* their children—that they should be healthy, wealthy, and wise, or the equivalent—but in expecting their children to work, parents in agrarian societies want considerably more *from* their children. These expectations die hard, so that even when they go to school, children in transitional societies (as we observed in Kenya and Mexico) are often expected to work at home in the many hours after school. Yet even in traditional agrarian settings, many of the child's activities at this age—including play and initiation ceremonies—lie outside parental control, suggesting that there are other influences on their children's development.

Responsibility

One of the most common parental expectations in agrarian societies is that older children will take care of an infant, often carrying him on their backs, comforting him when necessary, and feeding him as instructed—unsupervised by an adult. For modern American parents, this is somewhere between unlikely and unthinkable (as well as illegal): a six-year-old might be happy to amuse an infant for a while, but she is far from ready to care for one—or for that matter, to bear any of the responsibilities for useful work routinely expected of agrarian children. American parents regard these expectations as imposing inappropriate burdens on a child for the parents' own short-term benefit as opposed to providing for the older child's personal needs as a developing individual.

Mexico: Mayan Responsibility

In the field, we American and European observers, with our backgrounds in which children have long been freed from labor, are struck by the sight of children doing serious work. We are impressed with their relative maturity, and we ask questions about the processes by which they learn to do the tasks and about the emotions accompanying their sense of responsibility.

Among the Mayans of Yucatán, where men (assisted by boys) are primarily responsible for growing crops, the anthropologist Suzanne Gaskins reports that

> all children older than 1½ or two years are expected to do whatever chores they are asked to do quickly and effectively. The potential for work is constant, and the child is . . . a valuable participant in the household work activities.
>
> Beginning at age 6, children do a variety of household chores, run errands, help older siblings with chores beyond the compound, and take care of younger siblings. . . . The amount of time spent working . . . increases until it reaches approximately 60% by age 12 and continues there throughout the teenage years. . . . The early inclusion of children in work stems not only from need but also from a belief on the parents' part that chores help their children grow up to be competent and motivated workers. Thus, engaging children in adult work is responsible parenting.[3]

Learning to make tortillas is a priority for Mayan mothers of girls in the highlands of Guatemala and Chiapas (southern Mexico) as well as the lowlands of Yucatán (see photo insert).[4] It is a classic example of a complex task to which the home gives a young child visual access but which requires a proficiency that most girls achieve only in later childhood, at about nine years of age. And though the process may seem to involve learning *without* teaching—without verbal response—the mother's *judicious* (very restrained, from a Western point of view) use of language is critical to it.[5]

The "chore curriculum," as the anthropologist David Lancy calls it, is gender-specific, learned and practiced in family settings at ages ranging from eighteen months to marriage, and involves a progression to more difficult or responsible chores.[6] Agrarian children accept their subordinate roles. They imitate what they have observed their elders doing, often in pretend play, and for some tasks, as with the making of tortillas among the Mayans, the child may appear to *learn without being taught*. Indeed, in some agrarian communities, like the rice-growing Kpelle village in Liberia observed by Lancy, adults deliberately refrain from teaching their children.[7] In other communities, parents do teach their children, though their instruction is unlike that of a school classroom, as we show later.[8]

Kenya: The Changing Work of Gusii Children

The work expected of Gusii children changed over the thirty-two years (1956–1988) of our intermittent observations in one area. In the 1950s, before most Gusii children went to school, six- to eight-year-old Gusii girls were required to care for their infant siblings (see photo insert) and fetch water, and boys of that age herded sheep and goats (but not yet cows) to let them feed in pastures and keep them out of fields where crops were growing. If there were no girls in the family, infant care became the responsibility of an older brother of roughly the same age or the mother's younger sister, sent from her home. Children took care of an infant sibling when their mother was out in the fields planting, weeding, or harvesting or in the marketplace. The mother would strap the baby onto the child's back, giving the *omoreri* (caregiver) instructions for comforting the crying infant by jiggling first, then feeding gruel from a bottle. In those days, when fields were nearby and large and mothers—being responsible for the family's food supply—spent much time in cultivation, the caretaker would bring the baby to the mother in the field for breastfeeding, but by the 1970s mothers had smaller fields (growing tea, coffee, and pyrethrum for cash as well as food crops) and tended to come home more often. The children took their responsibilities seriously, and we rarely heard of any instance of neglect by an *omoreri*. Had there been an accident, the *omoreri* could have called on help from adults in nearby homesteads.

Thus, Gusii sibling caregiving involved real responsibility—by contemporary American standards, too much responsibility—for a six-year-old girl. But the problem with applying our standards is that we are thinking of *our* six-year-olds, who don't seem ready for it. We would say that a girl that age is too easily distracted, too devoted to her own playful interests, to be trusted with taking care of her baby brother all by herself. But Gusii girls by the age of six were observably different. Having grown up as compliant infants and toddlers without toys or other personal possessions, they had not acquired personal interests separate from those of the family, which were largely defined for them by mothers concerned with getting tasks done. Yes, they might have preferred to play rather than care for the baby, but they had learned to put their mother's task assignments first.

Fetching water also involved real responsibility, in this case, for the household's water supply. It required that a girl learn head-carrying: putting a grass ring on her head as a platform for a large ceramic pot, taking the pot down the hill empty, filling it with water from a stream, getting an adult woman to put the ring

and pot—now heavy with water—on her head, and carrying it up-
hill, often unsteadily, to the family house. Each pot had been purchased with cash from an itinerant Luo trader and was therefore
valuable, but it was also breakable, and the paths up the hill were
sometimes slippery, so the pressure on these girls, usually six to
eight years old, could be intense. Slipping and breaking a pot
would incur mother's ire and might result in a beating. Boys of
eleven or twelve who allowed the cows to trample or eat the crops
of nearby fields would also be beaten, by their fathers. Thus, children were entrusted with serious subsistence tasks carrying risks
that could result in punishment. Gusii mothers were stern task-
masters from an American perspective, and their children, perhaps fearing a scolding or punishment for wrongdoing, seemed
less playful and more subdued in mood than five- to nine-year-old
children we saw elsewhere in Africa. Mothers argued that they
had to be harsh with children that age to prepare them for their
initiation (girls at nine, boys at ten to eleven, described later in
this chapter).

These tasks assigned to children among the Gusii in the
1950s—caring for infants, fetching water, and shucking corn for
girls, tending animals and helping to construct houses for boys—
were similar to those found among the Kpelle and other rural
agriculturalists throughout the sub-Saharan region and among
many agrarian peoples elsewhere. But this would change in succeeding generations.

By the mid-1970s, twenty years later, all Gusii children, including girls, were attending school, and mothers could not count on
having a single seven-year-old daughter to care full-time for the
baby; instead, infant care came to be shared among the daughters
of the family, including teenagers. Families that now had wells
in their homesteads no longer depended on girls to bring water
from the stream, and the girls in families without wells now used

kerosene tins rather than breakable pots. With much less land—Gusii was now the densest rural area in Kenya—few families now had cattle, so boys were relieved of what had been a major responsibility, though they were still expected to do what they were told. In one generation, increased population density and universal schooling had drastically changed what Gusii parents expected from their children.

When we returned in 1988, another set of changes was visible: population growth had continued unabated, so few families could live by farming, and many of those with a secondary or higher education had left for Kenya's cities or migrated abroad. Those who remained in the rural area were poorer and less educated; some of the poorest had sold their land and lived off wages brought in by their school-age daughters, sent away to work as caregivers for the young children of affluent urbanites who promised to send the girls to school—a promise that reportedly was rarely fulfilled. The family as a domestic production team was a thing of the past.

The amount of responsibility expected of children before the spread of schooling varied across agrarian societies. Among the peoples we have examined, responsibility in childhood seemed to range from an extreme among the Yucatec Mayans, Gusii, and other African farmers to a more moderate level in India and Nepal, to a lower level still among some Pacific peoples, like the Manus studied by Mead.

India

In India there is variation by caste as well as rural-urban residence. Among traditional town-dwellers of Odiya (formerly Orissa), high-caste Hindu children work substantially less than not only other agrarian peoples but also their lower-caste counterparts. Lower-caste mothers are employed outside the home and leave the routine housework for their (unattended) children, as

Sarah also observed among the Dalits ("untouchables") of Andhra Pradesh. In other words, these children do the housework for the family without adult supervision. In urban Odiya, the anthropologist Susan Seymour reports, "responsible tasks" for children in the high-caste families include entertaining visitors rather than fetching water and the other onerous duties performed by low-caste children.[9]

Furthermore, many of the rural peoples of South Asia, like the Hindu farmers with whom we worked in Nepal, have technological advantages—like irrigation and ox-drawn plows (rare in sub-Saharan Africa)—that enable them to put less pressure on children to work than African parents did. The mother's workload, whether in employment, cultivation, or trading, is a key factor in determining how much time her children spend carrying out domestic responsibilities.[10] In the Pacific region, local communities with an abundance of fish or game collected by cooperative groups of men (like Margaret Mead's Manus) seem under far less pressure to use child labor in agriculture or work in general. Thus, ecological pressures, or their absence, play an important role in explaining the extent to which agrarian children are required to work.

Agrarian children's contribution to *domestic* production is not the child labor that horrified English and American reformers in the nineteenth century, when children worked in factories and mines. Nevertheless, there have been fairly horrifying late twentieth-century examples of children in agrarian societies employed outside the home, including the Gusii parents we mentioned who lived on their children's wages. But on a far larger scale, in India during the 1980s, there were some 17 million children working in match factories and potteries and on plantations. In his 1991 book *The Child and the State in India,* the political scientist Myron Weiner reports:

Child labor in India is largely a preindustrial, precapitalist labor force. Almost none of India's children work in mines or large factories, as was the case in England and the United States in the nineteenth century. India's children are mainly in the unorganized informal sector, including cottage industries and the tertiary service sector, or in agriculture. Child labor in India is not the product of industrialism and capitalism, but represents the persistence of the traditional role of the child as a worker.[11]

There is nonetheless a great difference between the working conditions of a child at home as a member of a farm family and those of a child toiling twelve hours a day in a factory where dangers are probably uncontrolled, and with additional hours of bus travel. That distinction often goes unrecognized in contemporary international efforts to abolish child labor in developing countries.

The Special Case of England

The movement to abolish child labor began in nineteenth-century England, where many children were working in factories and mines during the world's first industrial revolution. There were other unique conditions in England: by 1850 the majority of people were living in cities, and by 1870 only 14 percent of the population lived by agriculture. England was emerging more rapidly than other Western societies from the agrarian condition of household food production that depended heavily on children's contributions at home. But child labor *outside the home* was not new to England in the nineteenth century and in fact had unusually deep roots in traditions going back to the medieval period.

In preindustrial times, during the well-documented fifteenth to eighteenth centuries, the English were already living largely in nuclear family households rather than the large extended family households found in "peasant societies" of the same period in continental Europe. And even earlier, according to the historian-anthropologist Alan Macfarlane, in England, as of 1250,

> there were already a developed market and mobility of labor, land was treated as a commodity and full private ownership was established, there was very considerable geographical and social mobility, *a complete distinction between farm and family existed* [emphasis added], and rational accounting and the profit motive were widespread. . . . We could describe thirteenth-century England as a capitalist market economy without factories.[12]

It was in this singular context that sending children out to live and work in other families became an established practice. Why? The historian Ann Kussmaul reports that "larger farmers as well as small sent their sons and daughters into farm service."[13] Farmers who did not need the income sent their own children out to work elsewhere and replaced them at home with unrelated children or adolescents who could be more easily disciplined and might have more appropriate skills. In addition, these farmers believed that, by being sent out, their children could acquire working elsewhere skills and a sense of responsibility they could not get at home. There was clearly a notion that a parent's "sentimental" attachment to his or her child might interfere with being his employer, especially in discipline and avoidance of special treatment.

Sending children out of the home was institutionalized at all class levels. The poor sent their children out as servants, those better off (especially in towns) sent theirs to be apprentices in craft workshops (often paying a fee to the master), and the gentry sent theirs to boarding schools and to aristocratic households where they might acquire titled patrons. Boys were sent more often than girls, sometimes as young as seven years of age, but more often at eleven or twelve. Wage labor was widespread, and parents themselves were largely farm workers on large estates, artisans in craft workshops, or servants to privileged families. This was not the kind of setting for child rearing that we have found elsewhere in the agrarian world, and it laid a basis for the urban-industrial society England became 600 years later.

What kind of work did English children do? The historian Ralph Houlbrooke, in his overview of the English family from 1450 to 1700, presents the following picture of the economic contribution of the majority of children—that is, those not in the privileged classes—during later childhood:

> From about the age of eight onwards children were employed to weed, pick stones, gather wood, scare birds, mind babies, guard sheep, cast the seed in the furrow and help with harvest work. Children whose parents had no jobs for them to do would go to seek daywork from neighbors. In the seventeenth century, parents began to withdraw children from school as soon as they could make a useful economic contribution. The timing of the process largely depended upon the farmer's wealth; the greater a man's substance the longer he could leave his children there. Josiah Langdale (b. 1673) was not taken away till his father's death some time before he was nine. Then, a strong boy for his age, he was put to leading harrows, learning to plough and keeping the horse and oxen. William Stout (b. 1665) remembered how he and his brothers had begun to work rather later than his elder sister, who was soon needed to help her mother look after the younger children and to knit, sew and spin. As they reached ten or twelve, he and his brother were taken from school, especially in spring and summer, to look after the sheep, help with the plough, go with the cart for turves, make hay and take part in shearing.

In certain industries children began to work even earlier than in agriculture. In textile manufacture this was partly because the work could readily be performed under parental supervision and did not demand that much physical strength. Thomas Wilson, writing in 1601, observed that in English towns children were, from the age of six or seven, "forced to some art," whereby they maintained themselves and earned something for their parents and masters. In Norwich alone, so he claimed, children aged between six and ten had gained £12,000 a year, besides their keep, chiefly by knitting fine jersey stockings. In the early 1720s, Daniel Defoe, whose satisfaction concerning the employment of children resembled Wilson's, put the lower age of gainful employment of the properly taught child in textile areas at five around Taunton and Colchester, four or five around Norwich, and at four in the West Riding. But the 1570 Norwich census of the poor suggests that girls were much more readily fitted into the domestic economy of a textile town than were boys. Among those relatives whose age and sex were specified, over four-fifths of the girls were working, compared with less than a third of the boys. About a third of the boys were still at school. Lacking as yet the strength to play a useful part in male work, only a minority of these boys were entrusted with female work such as spinning and knitting which employed a substantial majority of the girls.[14]

But there weren't jobs enough for all the children, Houlbrooke reports, so local authorities put all begging children over five to service.

Houlbrooke emphasizes the love of parents for their children and the concern for their welfare even when they were living separately. Yet there is no doubt that sending children to live, work, and study outside the parental home was institutionalized in preindustrial England, that many children in the five-to-ten age range were sent out as participants in the paid labor force, and that parental concern for their offspring had to be expressed at a distance. It is also clear that children at home participated in household food production under parental supervision at ages comparable to other agrarian societies, until they were sent away.

Yet centuries later England led the way in abolishing child labor, breaking sharply with a long-standing tradition in which parents could consider themselves devout Christians while sending their children to live and labor (full-time) elsewhere for pecuniary gain. The intervening period, roughly 1750 to 1872, saw the rise not only of an industrial capitalism that exploited children on a large scale but also of a countervailing Romantic movement in literature that conceptualized children as innocents to be protected and a middle-class political reform movement that translated those concerns into collective action. Laws were enacted, children's school attendance without labor became the norm, and the moral attitudes of parents were fundamentally changed.

England was a complex society: although reforms took place, its monarchy and most of its aristocratic traditions were not abolished. Sending out children, though associated with factory labor in the lower strata of society, was an aspect of privilege among the aristocracy and gentry, who continued to send their boys to well-known boarding schools ("public schools," some dating from the Middle Ages) with others of their class. Since many of those in the upper classes lived on country estates rather than in the city or were serving abroad in the military or colonial service, they also found boarding schools convenient. By 1900, boarding schools were also becoming normative for girls from upper-class families.

It never occurred to Sarah's parents not to send her to a private school. Boarding school was a given also. Sarah's father had gone, and her mother—who was tutored at home by a series of French and German governesses before going to be "finished" in Paris at age seventeen—deeply regretted that she had not. Like her brother and sister, from age four Sarah attended a nearby day school, with twenty children and three teachers in a spacious country house that provided elementary education for sons and daughters of the local gentry. Her brother left for "prep" school at eight and then moved on to public school at thirteen. Sarah, at eleven, followed her sister to a girls' boarding school that focused on music, the arts, team sports, and making friends to last a lifetime. The school was located in a stately home whose owners had no longer been able to afford to live there after World War II and had sold it to the school for a song. Approached by a half-mile-long drive, the school was surrounded by wide lawns, water gardens, a walled garden containing a swimming pool, an immense kitchen garden, and a park in which cattle and sheep grazed. The ballroom doubled as chapel and dance studio. Every student was permitted to take one pet to school. After much thought, Sarah's sister decided to leave her pony at home and take her rabbit; Sarah also left her pony at home and took her tortoise instead. Following four lightly academic and mostly pleasant years, Sarah moved on to a second, more academic girls' boarding school to prepare for university entrance. At each school she made one lifelong friend, each of whom, like Sarah, strayed far from the ruling class in adulthood. Both schools offered scholarships to a scattering of gifted girls from less privileged families. The rest regarded these scholarship girls, who didn't speak with quite the same accent, used a slightly different vocabulary, disliked team sports, and didn't know how to ride, with a mixture of awe and condescension. As for the scholarship girls, whether or not they flourished academically, socially they rarely felt that they belonged.

Did those of Sarah's generation who had gone to boarding school wish they had not? Many remembered being horribly homesick, at least to start with, and a good many boys remember being beaten for minor infractions and sexually preyed upon, usually by older boys but sometimes by teachers. (Girls seem to have suffered much less abuse than boys did. Though Sarah remembers being threatened with a riding crop, she was never actually beaten, and no older girl or teacher showed the least sexual interest in her.) Yet for the most part they thought the rewards outweighed the suffering and deprivation, and when their own children reached school age they tended to send them to boarding schools. (By the 1980s parental visiting days were more numerous, midterm breaks were lengthening, and many public schools were accepting girls in the upper grades.) Likewise, today's British upper-class parents feel honor-bound to give their children every advantage they can afford, and boarding school— which costs roughly $50,000 a year—is still regarded as the ne plus ultra of privilege.

Child Labor in the American Farm Family

On the nineteenth-century American frontier, as the historian Steven Mintz relates, children:

> provided game and wild plants for their families' tables as well as the fuel to cook their food. They cut hay, herded cattle and sheep, burned brush, gathered eggs, and churned butter. They also broke sod, planted, weeded, and harvested. Farmers on the plains could not afford to delay their offspring's entry into the family workforce. A Kansas father bragged that his two-year-old son could "fetch up cows out of the stock fields, or oxen, carry in stove wood and climb in the corn crib and feed the hogs and go

on errands." Improved plows and other farm machinery allowed young sons and daughters to assist with plowing, planting and harvesting. An Oklahoma father gave each of his children a knife to hack the soil and "make a seed bed for a garden and the first crop of kaffir corn." Fannie Eisele was only ten years old when she began to plow her family's Oklahoma fields.[15]

Whatever we may think of it today, the child labor of the American farm family in the nineteenth century or the Gusii, Mayan, or Kpelle family in the 1950s was distinctly different from child labor in factories and mines in several important respects—in working hours, in the supervision by a caring parent, in the amount of risk involved, and in other conditions. Yet distinguishing clearly between the two in legislation was often difficult: parents were usually the ones responsible for putting children into labor when they worked for pay outside the home, and children who worked at home part of the time sometimes also took jobs outside. Furthermore, did it make sense to ban factory employment for fourteen-year-olds while leaving that Kansas father free to direct his two-year-old to "climb in the corn crib and feed the pigs"? Finally, once public school attendance became the compulsory alternative to child labor, it was probably inevitable that the state would increasingly take from parents the power to set standards for the treatment of children.

However desirable the abolition of child labor is in the abstract or in extreme cases of large-scale exploitation, observations in agrarian families show children not only enjoying their chores and spontaneously performing tasks above the expectations for their age but also finding time to play while attending to chores, even in Africa and other places where children make essential contributions to domestic production. David Lancy's monograph about the hardworking Kpelle children in Liberia has chapters on the same children's pretend play, games, dancing, singing, and storytelling.[16]

Learning at Home and in School

Children learn a huge amount during later childhood, from parents and siblings and from the observation of others. Parents in agrarian societies without schools organize their children's learning experiences as training in responsible tasks. In assuming responsibility for the care of an infant or for the family's water supply or livestock, a child learns not only the knowledge necessary to get the job done but a good deal more as well. Responsibility training is moral education as well as the acquisition of intellectual skills.

China

In China, parents are guided by an ancient ideology that leads them to see themselves as their children's first teachers and engage them in didactic instruction in morality and habits of mind they believe will help later in school; in such a context, the child's learning goes far beyond task training.

When it comes to learning, the Chinese are in certain respects a special case. China was, of course, an agrarian society, perhaps the largest one in world history, but unlike those of sub-Saharan Africa, it had long had a tradition of literacy, urban centers, and a centralized political system. During most of China's history, its population was largely made up of illiterate peasants, but they were governed by an emperor who had an elaborate court and bureaucracy. Officials in the bureaucracy were drawn from a literate class of scholars who were venerated for their learning by everyone, including the peasants of the countryside. Thus, Chinese traditions, as represented by their popular culture, portrayed scholars, literacy, academic learning, and formal examinations as worthy of the highest regard, even though only a small proportion of people were actually involved. Recent centuries have seen the movement of Chinese overseas to Taiwan, Hong Kong, and Singapore, as well as to cities in the eastern part of the Chinese mainland, where Western-type schooling was adopted. It was also adopted for all of mainland China by Mao Zedong's Communist republic, so that by the late twentieth century China had become the country with the largest number of children attending school.

We don't have observations of parenting in rural Chinese families and communities in the old agrarian times before the spread of schooling. We do have a number of accounts of parenting in Chinese urban and rural communities where schooling is well established, as well as studies of Chinese immigrants in the United States and Canada. In all these cases, parents not only are deeply attached to traditional Chinese concepts of learning but also see them as applicable to their children's performance in Western-type schools. These traditional concepts, usually based on Confucian texts of 2,500 years ago, mix learning with moral virtue and endow school learning with morality in a blend that is distinctly Chinese. The anthropologist Charles Stafford reports from an isolated fishing village in southeastern Taiwan that in the fifth year of school children read a text that states, "Studying (*qiuxue*) and being a person (*zuoren*) are inseparable."[7] Stafford emphasizes that texts like this make explicit what is "common sense" to everyone, including parents. The school texts even feed back into family relations by emphasizing how much children owe their mothers and fathers. In this village, many parents, especially mothers, who actually had little or no schooling themselves were supportive of their children's educational careers, though they participated less in school activities than parents in urban areas.

In the urban places where they have been observed, Chinese parents operate with an explicit code of teaching and learning based on those Confucian texts. The psychologist Jin Li outlines the seven Confucian "learning virtues": sincerity, diligence, endurance of hardship, perseverance, concentration, respect for teachers, and humility.[18] They might sound to an American like a level of dedication more appropriate to a priest than a pupil in school. The term "diligence" is particularly revealing of cultural difference. For Chinese parents, diligence is crucial, virtuous, and a source of pride—a child should be diligent in school. If an American mother is told that her Johnny is a diligent learner, she might think she's being told that her son is a drudge, lacking in initiative, independence, and creativity. Even allowing for ambiguity in translation (although "diligence" is the standard translation of *qinfen*), the contrast is telling. As Li says, "Diligence is the virtue that underlies frequent, constant, studious behavior. It emphasizes much time spent on learning."[19] Chinese parents expect it.

No wonder the children of Chinese immigrants do well in school here in North America! Chinese parents consider the child's development as a moral person to be intertwined with, and dependent on, learning and school performance. They don't expect school to be fun, and they routinely criticize their children without worrying about harming the child's self-esteem. They strive to inculcate humility, so that their children are less boisterous than their American peers.

Middle-class American parents are also likely to see themselves as teachers as they train their toddlers, and even their infants, in the question-and-answer routines of the classroom long before the children actually enter one. Conversing with their children, they are good at building the vocabulary skills that are valued in the early grades of American schools. But they also strive to inculcate independence, autonomy, and initiative, re-gardless of schooling, which they consider separate from other aspects of the child's life and behavior. These American goals, in contrast with the Chinese emphasis on obedience and diligence, may not lead to better performance in school, which American parents see as only one of several arenas for achievement (sports being another).

What Children Learn

Children are avid, inveterate learners whose learning—everywhere—is not confined to parentally organized instruc-tions or training routines. Children in agrarian societies acquire environmental knowledge—like the names of wild plants and whether they are edible, poisonous, or medicinal, and practical knowledge, like how to plant crops—long before parents instruct them. (In the 1950s we encountered among the Gusii a pair of twin girls only six years old who had persuaded their mother to let them plant a small plot of corn, which they weeded and har-vested, to the family's satisfaction.) Children also absorb a wide variety of folk beliefs from peers, older siblings, and grandpar-ents, whether or not anyone tries to teach them. As they acquire a larger vocabulary during these years, they can talk about more things, persons, and relationships, and as they mature cognitively they gain the ability to organize their knowledge more effectively.

Sending children to school was a major historical threshold for parents as well as children. For parents, as mentioned, compul-sory education meant giving up control over their children's ac-tivities. For children, it meant learning in a new place outside the home, standardized in its spatial organization and communication, taught by an adult outside the family whom they were told to re-spect as an authoritative figure. This was normally the first contact children had with bureaucratic institutions in their society. The content they had to learn (the curriculum) was as standardized as the method of delivering it, and it became the shared experience of children of diverse backgrounds. In many agrarian societies during the second half of the twentieth century, standardization often began with the learning of the national language in school. A Gusii schoolchild (whose first language was Ekegusii) learned Swahili, the lingua franca of Kenya, and English; a Mayan schoolchild (whose first language might be Yucatec Mayan) learned Spanish; and a rural school child in Nepal, a country with dozens of ethnic groups speaking different languages, learned Nepali, the national language, along with the format of bureaucratic schooling, in which a strange adult instructs children through speech rather than the imitation-participation of the agrarian family.

By the last decades of the twentieth century, however, the life of an urban elementary school-aged child in a transitional society differed greatly from a rural child's. Families were smaller than in the countryside and, while children—girls especially—might be expected to perform domestic tasks after school hours, there were no animals to care for, fields to weed, wheat to thresh, or maize kernels to grind. Attending school had become the work of childhood. After-school hours were spent doing homework and light household chores; once those were finished, children were free to play or watch TV, now almost ubiquitous. If the household included a teenage girl, either a daughter or a niece who had finished school and was "waiting to get married," she would be most likely to do the necessary chores, thereby freeing her younger siblings and cousins to do as they pleased. In cities like Kathmandu, Ndola, and Cuernavaca and in small market towns like Tilzapotla and Kisii, children were on the way to being—like their American age-mates—bearers of parental hopes.

Control: Corporal Punishment in
England, America, and Elsewhere

Nothing divides us from our agrarian ancestors as much as whether—and how—to punish children when they are five to ten years old. Our ancestors considered beating (smacking, thrashing, or slapping at home, caning in school) a necessary moral discipline to prevent sin and improve godliness; we consider it physical abuse that is immoral and can be illegal. Yet the transition in the English-speaking world was surprisingly gradual and continued until recently.

On the agrarian side, few peoples actually *prohibited* beating or slapping a child; although the otherwise easygoing Trobrianders described by Malinowski were said to have beaten their children (and children also slapped their parents), physical punishment was not necessarily frequent among agrarian peoples. Parents often assumed that a threat was more effective than the action, that the *possibility* of a beating would lead a child to avoid disapproved behavior. Contemporary Americans might claim that even physical threats tarnish the parent-child relationship and add an immoral element of coercion or terror that simply shouldn't be there, so the mere fact that agrarian parents rarely did what they occasionally threatened would not make it more acceptable to us.

Does physical punishment still go on? The sociologist Murray Straus reported in 2009:

> Provided the child is not physically injured in a way that leaves lasting marks or bruises, parental use of corporal punishment is legal in every state in the United States and until recently was legal in all other countries.

Studies in the United States and England have found that more than a third of parents inflict corporal punishment on infants at least once and more than 90% spank toddlers. From age 6 onward, the rate decreases rapidly, but a 1995 US national survey found that a third of parents of 13-year-old children were still using physical force to control the children's behavior. Until recently, corporal punishment by teachers was equally prevalent.[20]

According to Straus, the worldwide movement to end corporal punishment by parents and in schools began in 1979, which UNESCO designated the International Year of the Child. Governments, beginning with Sweden that year, outlawed a practice that was once the preferred way to discipline children. The British Parliament banned caning in schools by a close vote (231–230) on July 23, 1986; the ban applied only to government-subsidized schools. (Private schools did not follow until 1998.) As the *New York Times* reported at the time:

> Most officials of the Thatcher Government voted to retain caning as a teacher's option, but 35 Conservatives voted no. . . . The fact that it was still practiced was brought home on the day of the debate by articles about a small boy who displayed a badly bruised backside said to have been sustained in a caning. Opponents of abolition noted that the boy attended a private school not covered by the ban. . . . The vote will bring Britain into line with the rest of Europe.[21]

Corporal punishment had actually been declining, though unevenly, among Western countries during the second half of the twentieth century, with more "progressive" segments of societies in the lead and more conservative segments, like private schools in Britain, lagging behind. History records the laws on the books but not the number of beatings that took place. But we know that in the end, despite complaints by a minority who would like to bring it back, corporal punishment is deeply disapproved, especially by child care professionals and their organizations.

In Gusiiland in the 1970s, Sarah would often hear a mother threatening to beat her child who had misbehaved, but she never saw one doing so. And though homesteads were close enough together for her to hear whatever might be going on, she never heard a child screaming. Physically violent behavior was perpetrated only by men who fought after drinking beer or came home drunk to beat their wives or adolescent offspring. In Mexico, too, Sarah found domestic abuse of wives by their drunken husbands to be common, but children were rarely beaten.

Ritual Transitions and Secret Societies

Preindustrial England was not the only society in which parents lost, or voluntarily relinquished, control over their older children. In the forest region of West Africa (particularly Liberia, Sierra Leone, and Guinea), the Poro and Sande "societies" socialized boys and girls (separately) in the bush outside the village. Down the eastern side of Africa, from Ethiopia to South Africa, there were many peoples who had initiation ceremonies, often involving ritual circumcision and clitoridectomy followed by a period of gender-specific training in seclusion (from parents and other adults) and then a public ceremonial graduation to adult status. Some of these societies, like the Maasai of Kenya and Tanzania, also had an age-set organization into which boys were inducted and through which they became men and then elders; this organization operated separately from the families and kinship groups of their members.

Initiation ceremonies for older children or adolescents, with or without genital operations, are also found outside of Africa, in aboriginal Australia, New Guinea, and Native North America. Many of the societies with initiation rituals are nonliterate, lack political organization beyond the local community, and—perhaps surprisingly—are geographically close to societies that have *no* such rituals. It appears that initiation ceremonies play an important role in giving these stateless peoples a distinctive ethnic identity that can be mobilized in warfare, and genital operations mark off "us" from "them." The boys so marked become the warriors to fight against those who lack marks.

In much of Eurasia, parents also experienced limits on their control of their older children as they followed the instructions of clerics—Hindu, Buddhist, Muslim, Catholic, Protestant, and Jewish—in implementing religious ideals prescribed in scripture. The ritual transition to adulthood—as in the Hindu sacred thread ceremony, Christian first communion, and Jewish bar mitzvah—gives dramatic form to the child's attainment of moral maturity. Parents play a supporting, distinctly secondary role.

Parents do not choose the moral curriculum of transition rites, but they can play an important role in helping to prepare the child for them. In the Gusii initiation ceremonies, for example, parents play no part in the seclusion that follows the male circumcision, when older youth give the novices a brief training course in adult behavior—focused on warrior ideals and the morality of mother-son avoidance. But unlike the boys, the girls are secluded in their mother's house, and though the ritual is conducted by older girls, older women may also participate. The parents have done their work in advance, making it clear to children of both sexes that they must be brave in the face of the painful operation, which means making no sound at all for the ten- to eleven-year-old boys and not screaming or running away for the eight- to nine-year-old girls. They have been told that it would not only disgrace the family but also offend the ancestral spirits, with dreadful consequences. Parents see the ability to restrain themselves in these ways as demonstrating an adult level of moral maturity. (Before the British conquest in 1907, both boys and girls were teenagers when they were circumcised.) Before their circumcision, boys are expected to show that they can tolerate separation from their mothers by sleeping in a nearby house and that they have become modest by wearing shorts that cover their genitals; these acts demonstrate their readiness for the mother-son avoidance that will follow their initiation. Mothers supervise the preparatory behaviors of both boys and girls and warn them that they will not be allowed to be circumcised with their peers if they don't behave responsibly (for example, if a girl fails to perform a chore that she will be relieved of after initiation). The parents, in other words, work on the motivation of their children, using the threat of not joining their age-mates in the initiation ritual if they do not begin conforming to the adult moral code.

Gusii parents put their offspring through these ordeals, they say, to ensure that the children will be recognized in the community as complete adults—as warriors if they are boys and as desirable wives and mothers if they are girls. Gusii are keenly aware that the neighboring Luo people do not practice circumcision for either sex, and they will say (if asked by an outsider) that the Luo remain children forever. Whether or not they believe this, there is no question that they feel superior to people who lack these customs and that initiation practices are centrally involved in their identity as Gusii. The contrast buttresses the cultural identities of groups on both sides, giving them a sense of solidarity within their own group and making them feel superior to the others.

The whole idea of genital surgery performed on an eight-year-old girl by a folk practitioner is anathema to Americans, as it was to the Scottish and Anglican missionaries who encountered it in central Kenya early in the twentieth century. By 1928, it had already given rise to the conflict between missionaries and the Kikuyu people that would emerge as the Mau Mau Rebellion in the 1950s. The custom cannot be understood, let alone justified, without immersion in the culture of the people who practice it. If anthropology means seeing customs "from the native's point of view," as Malinowski put it ninety years ago, this particular custom—defended by Malinowski's student Jomo Kenyatta in his book *Facing Mount Kenya* (1938)—pushes our empathy to its limit or beyond.[22] Different forms of female genital surgery are practiced across a wide area of northeastern Africa, including Egypt and Somalia, always as a required step toward adulthood. In Muslim countries of the region—Sudan, Somalia, and Egypt—it is often believed to be a Koranic requirement, though that is not accepted elsewhere.

For decades now, there has been an international campaign against female genital mutilation (FGM), or female genital cutting, as part of feminist and human rights agendas. United Nations agencies, including UNICEF and UNFPA (the UN Population Fund), have joined the campaign, emphasizing health risks as well as human rights violations. In 2011 Kenya's parliament passed a law, the Prohibition of Female Genital Mutilation Act, which also established an enforcement agency, but as recently as 2014 it was reported that FGM had a prevalence of 96 percent among the Gusii. Yet Kenya as a whole reported a decline of 6.6 percent in FGM from 2005 to 2010, prior to the legislation,

suggesting that there was a trend toward abandoning the practice. Female genital operations, another example of a practice
grounded in local morality that puts children's health at risk and
offends the moral sensibilities of Westerners, may well disappear
before the end of this century.

Conclusions

In this chapter, we have examined some of the ways in which
parents in diverse cultures manage older children's lives, activities, and development. In addition to the great divide between
agrarian parents organizing their children for production at home
and modern parents sending their children to school (with many
societies now in transition as schooling spreads), there are surprising variations: for example, in some agrarian societies parents assume the role of teacher while in others parents expect
children to learn from example. They also vary in whether and
how much they permit children to play, and in whether there are
ritual initiations and transitions that parents support but do not
manage.

We found that the amount of pressure on children to work
at home varied widely across the agrarian world, depending on
the abundance of wild food (fish, game, roots) and the use of
agricultural technologies; both the plow and irrigation reduce the
need for child labor and give children more time for play. Perhaps our greatest surprise was finding how exceptional parents in
preindustrial England were in routinely sending their older children to work in other people's households and craft workshops.
In West Africa, children are often fostered with relatives; in the
Pacific, they are often adopted by kin or others. In recent times,
some major historical transitions—urbanization and the spread
of Western-type schools—have also decreased parental control

and child labor contributions even in predominantly agrarian countries. In addition, there is an international trend toward less corporal punishment.

If we focus on worldwide trends, we can find them, but the lives of older children remain highly variable across the world. No dimension of variation is more striking than agrarian parents' expectations of respect and obedience from children as they approach puberty as well as in their early years.

~ 8 ~

Precocious Children:
Cultural Priming by Parents and Others

THE PRECOCIOUSNESS OF children is in the eye of the beholder. A child prodigy in mathematics or music is recognized as a rarity in our society, but when we look across cultures, we see many young children doing amazingly skillful, mature, and sometimes risky things that are rare here at home: handling and operating knives and plows, caring for babies, and capably taking care of themselves and others. Like our agrarian ancestors, they assume responsibilities at an age when our contemporary children are still dependent on their parents. They're not prodigies, but they are certainly precocious by our standards. Many of the tasks assigned to children in agrarian contexts—particularly work and infant care—have long been banned by law in our society, but agrarian children also take care of themselves without help from adults—which is not illegal—at an earlier age than our contemporary children.

Modern societies also vary in the ways their children are precocious, contrasting with their American counterparts. In France, children are polite to adults at an earlier age than we expect it, and as the title of a recent book tells us, *French Kids Eat Everything,* in contrast with the picky eaters we are accustomed to.[1] Young Japanese children, as described later in this chapter, are surprisingly empathic. These cultural patterns of precocity reflect not only parental priorities but also the control that parents have over children during their earliest years, when they are acquiring a first language and learning to participate in the cultural routines of the home.

The evidence from diverse cultures, both agrarian and modern, permits us to see surprising—and instructive—examples of precocious children in action.

Self-Reliance:
Americans, Germans, and Matsigenkans

American parents want their children to grow up to be independent and self-reliant, and their sleeping arrangements reflect that priority. It may not seem possible that infants and children in some other cultures could be even *more* self-reliant than Americans, but there are striking examples to suggest just that.

Take, for example, babies in the city of Bielefeld in northwest Germany in the 1970s. Research conducted there at that time revealed infant care practices that not only were reported to exceed the "independence" sought by American parents but also had a pronounced effect on the babies' behavior by ten months of age. The study of forty-nine infants conducted in Bielefeld by the child psychologists Karin and Klaus Grossmann and their collaborators was designed as a replication of Mary Ainsworth's classic study of twenty-six middle-class infants and mothers in

Baltimore, Maryland.[2] Like the Baltimore study, it included home observations during the first year. The Grossmanns found that when the Bielefeld one-year-olds, in an experiment called the Strange Situation, were separated briefly from their mothers, almost half of them (49 percent) did *not* seek comfort from their mothers on their return, whereas in Baltimore only 26 percent responded that way. To explain the difference, the Grossmanns report that in northern Germany

> People tend to keep a larger interpersonal distance. As soon as infants become mobile, most mothers feel that they should now be weaned from close bodily contact. To carry a baby who can move on its own or to respond to its every cry by picking it up would be considered as spoiling. The ideal is an independent, nonclinging infant who does not make demands on the parents but rather unquestioningly obeys their commands.

They found that even the mothers of "securely attached" infants "offered a toy in response to their infants' distress signals about three times as often as Baltimore mothers . . . , thus diverting the infants from close bodily proximity. They often tried to relieve the infants' distress by other means than picking them up, which was quite successful in many instances."[3]

The Grossmanns also point out that the attachment category considered by Ainsworth to indicate a baby's *optimal* security— "securely attached"—"would be judged by many German parents as that of a spoiled or immature toddler."[4] Furthermore:

> The mothers never failed to comment upon their children's ability to play by themselves, and upon whether they were satisfied with the extent to which their babies were able to play alone. It was a reason for complaining if their infants always needed

company or wanted to be entertained. Many mothers were concerned that they would spoil their infants if they reacted to every cry of his or hers, but they usually made sure that nothing "serious" was the matter. Crying for company was not considered "serious."[5]

Most telling are the Grossmanns' home observations when the babies were ten months old. They found that the Bielefeld infants cried only 6.7 percent of the time when their mothers left the room, whereas the Baltimore infants cried 18 percent of the time. The Baltimore infants greeted the mother positively when she entered the room 33 percent of the time, but the Bielefeld infants did so only 18.2 percent of the time. And the Baltimore infants initiated a pick-up 18.4 percent of the time and made a positive response to it 26 percent of the time, while the Bielefeld infants did so 6.7 percent of the time, responding positively 13.3 percent of the time.[6] The German babies at ten months, in other words, had already been conditioned to conform to their mothers' desire for less "dependent" children. To prevent the development of the kind of "spoiled" and "immature" infant that Americans (including psychologists) see as "optimal," the Bielefeld mothers were successful in producing babies whose greater independence *at ten months* was evident in home observations. This would seem to be a clear case of culture-specific precocity during the first year of life.

But how sure can we be that behavioral differences between forty-nine Bielefeld infants observed in 1977 and twenty-three Baltimore infants observed in 1964 mean that Germans as a whole differ from Americans in general? Not very—the findings are suggestive but call for replications. The Grossmanns' replication study in southwestern Germany (Regensburg, Bavaria) showed much less difference from Baltimore, and later studies in

Los Angeles turned up American mothers who, valuing infant independence, had attitudes indistinguishable from those of their Bielefeld counterparts.[7] Large, complex, and changing modern societies like Germany and the United States are bound to show variations by region and social class as well as generation. No single small-scale study can be taken to represent the entire population, not even at a particular moment in time.

The Bielefeld-Baltimore comparison nevertheless shows that mothers with a set of cultural ideals differing from those of middle-class Americans can produce precociously independent infants—by American standards—during the first year. This remains an impressive result, even though the cultural ideals of both societies have changed over the last thirty years. We Americans are not necessarily raising the most independent children in the modern world!

What about the agrarian world, where infant care favors "interdependence" over independence? Is it possible that there are examples of precocious independence even there? The anthropologists Elinor Ochs and Carolina Izquierdo argue that the self-reliance of toddlers is intertwined with their responsibility training among agrarian peoples, as illustrated, from Izquierdo's fieldwork, by a girl named Yanira from the Matsigenka people of the Peruvian Amazon:

> Yanira stood waiting with a small pot and a bundle with two dresses and a change of underwear in hand. She asked to accompany the anthropologist and a local family on a fishing and leaf gathering expedition down river. Over five days away from the village, Yanira was self-sufficient and attuned to the needs of the group. She helped to stack and carry leaves to bring back to the village for roofing. Mornings and late afternoons she swept sand off the sleeping mats, fished for slippery black crustaceans,

cleaned and boiled them in her pot along with manioc, then served them to the group. At night her cloth bundle served as blanket and her dresses as pillows. Calm and self-possessed, she asked for nothing. Yanira was six years old.[8]

Ochs and Izquierdo point out that agrarian parents who emphasize respect and obedience also expect children to take care of themselves earlier than middle-class Americans do. Yanira's self-sufficiency, they claim, is not exceptional among agrarian societies. We see Yanira as particularly precocious at six only because we expect so much less self-sufficiency from our own six-year-olds. As American parents burden themselves by doing for their children what the children can do for themselves, they may also be depriving their children of valuable training in self-reliance as well as responsibility. Ochs and Izquierdo suggest that it is entirely possible to have children who routinely perform responsible tasks as well as play and learn.[9] American parents, on the other hand, contradict their own stated aims and cast doubt on the independence-interdependence dichotomy. We discuss Ochs and Izquierdo's critique of middle-class American parenting at greater length in our final chapter.

Precocious American Talkers

American children at two to three years old are reputedly precocious speakers, treasured by adults for their early facility in speaking and engaging them in conversation. This reflects American middle-class parents' hope that their children will speak as early as possible, their practice of speaking to their children frequently from birth onwards and engaging them in emotionally exciting face-to-face mock conversations and play dialogues even before they can speak, and their support for the expansion of their children's vocabulary once they begin to acquire language. As we argued in Chapter 7, toddlers also learn the conventions for using language in their culture.

We don't know whether American preschool children actually have better conversational abilities than, say, French children or just *lack* the social skill to restrain their speech in adult contexts, as French children do. The second alternative seems more likely, but only empirical research can decide. From the American point of view, French children are *precociously restrained* and adultlike, but from the perspectives of many peoples outside the United States, American middle-class children are *precociously talkative*. Precocity is a judgment reached by comparing the observed behavior of a child outside her own group with a reference standard shaped by the age-linked behavior of children at home.

As if to prove that the American penchant for precocious communication changes with technology, we have the case of three-year-old Aryanna Lynch. As reported in the *Boston Globe* in March 2014, Aryanna's mother, Tiffany Lynch, who was eight months pregnant,

> woke up one morning . . . with a vicious stomach bug. She made her daughters breakfast and went into the living room, where she remembers doubling over in nausea. But then her mind went blank. The expectant mother had collapsed and was unconscious.
>
> Her 3-year-old daughter, Aryanna, grabbed her mother's cellphone off the floor and, somehow, unlocked the screen. Then she found a picture of her cousin, pressed it to call her, and left a message.
>
> "Come over," she told her cousin.
>
> Her cousin called the police and dialed Aryanna back immediately, and the little girl answered the phone, terrified and

crying. Four police cruisers, a fire truck, and an ambulance showed up at their Abbott Street home, and Aryanna, dressed up as Snow White, her favorite Disney princess, unlocked the front door to let the rescuers in.[10]

Children in some places are raised speaking more than one language, and their bilingual or multilingual development can start at the time children elsewhere are learning a first language. Children growing up bilingual seem precocious in that respect, but they also pose unresolved problems concerning the acquisition of cultural meanings: which language's meanings become part of the child's psychological makeup and which do not? This question could be studied in many parts of the world where we and our students and colleagues have worked, ranging from Nepal, Kenya, and Zambia to Gambia and other parts of the West African coast, where children grow up learning at least two languages and often more, one of them being the national language in which schooling is conducted.

There are other unanswered questions about language precocity in the young child. For example, the psycholinguist Twyla Tardif has shown that while two-year-olds learning English or other European languages as their first language know more nouns than verbs, Chinese children of that age, learning Mandarin or Cantonese, know more verbs (or verblike words) than nouns.[11] Does this mean that the Chinese children are better able to talk about action and European or American children about things?

Many of the most interesting studies of what young children think in Western sites ranging from Geneva to Berkeley are *dependent* on the precocious willingness of children in those places to carry on a conversation with an adult. Investigators in some other places have to devise strategies to overcome the resistance to talking with adults that young children may have acquired as part of their early language learning.

Japan: Empathy

Japanese children have been repeatedly described by observers as capable of considering the feelings of others at an early age. In discussing a Japan-US comparative study in which he collaborated in the 1970s, Hiroshi Azuma, a leading Japanese child psychologist, revealed that, of the Japanese mothers who were interviewed in the study about how they responded to a (three-year-old) child's refusal to eat certain vegetables at dinner, about 10 percent reported that they said, "Okay, you don't have to"—at which point the child *ate the vegetables*.[12] Azuma and his team in Japan interpreted the child's behavior as a response to an implicit threat that the mutually dependent relationship between mother and child (*amae* in Japanese) would be cut off. But why would the child interpret the mother's concession as a threat? To understand this we have to go back to the observations of the psychologist Shusuke Kobayashi as described in our introduction. Recall that the Japanese mothers of two-year-olds never stopped their sweet pleadings in the face of their child's opposition or misbehavior. That experience seems to lead a child to interpret the rare instance of his mother giving in as a threat to terminate her affectionate support. Who would have thought so? Not Azuma's American collaborators, whom he had to convince that he understood Japanese three-year-olds better than they did. But this shows the subtleties that can be involved in a child's early communications. And it suggests that Japanese children are attuned, perhaps precociously, to the feelings of their mothers.

A major goal of the Japanese mother is for her toddler to learn *omoiyari,* roughly translatable as "empathy." Mothers bring the potential feelings of others into conversations with their young children. In observations of dinnertime narratives, Misako Tsutsui Steveron found that the mother "implicitly teaches her child how to express feelings and how to empathize with other's feelings by mentioning the child's feelings toward the central event of the narrative."[3] Some of Azuma's Japanese mothers in the old comparative study told their children that the farmer who grew the vegetable, or even the vegetable itself, would be sad if they didn't eat it. We witnessed that strategy in our own house when we had a Japanese mother and her four-year-old son living with us for a few months. The mother was a graduate student, and the child had been raised speaking English as well as Japanese, so we could understand when she tried to convince him to eat his vegetables with an appeal to his pity for the farmer and the vegetables themselves.

More recently, the education researcher and Japan specialist Joseph Tobin and his collaborators have written of "the pedagogy of *sabishii,*" which means "sad/lonely," in a preschool in Kyoto:

> The classroom teacher, circulating around the room, notices that many of the children have finished their meat and rice and dessert, but left their carrots untouched. Speaking to a boy in a theatrical voice loud enough for the whole class to hear, the teacher says "Poor Mister Carrot! You ate Mr. Hamburger and Mr. Rice, but you haven't eaten any of Mr. Carrot. Don't you think he feels *sabishii*?"[14]

As the anthropologist of Japan George DeVos writes: "The child is made aware of his potential to hurt objects and people. This is a form of moral inculcation, rather than a tempering of contentious wills, as characterizes parent-child interaction in the United States. Japanese children are quickly made sensitive to their capacity to arouse negative feelings in others."[5]

Does *sabishii* pedagogy have an effect? A comparative study of Japanese and American children in fourth and fifth grades found that in response to questions about children's fighting, more of the Japanese showed "awareness of the psychological or physical needs of another individual or awareness of the psychological or physical consequences . . . ('It would hurt him')," and that a Japanese child "takes the perspective of a third person observing the situation and identifies feelings of empathy or sympathy (e.g., 'I would feel sad if I saw a child being teased')."[6] Insofar as Japanese ten- to eleven-year-olds are precociously empathic by comparison with Americans, it would seem that the *sabishii* pedagogy of the mother and the preschool has made a difference. In this Japanese instance, however, the mother's teaching of the toddler is explicitly supported by preschool teachers.

Our own observations in Nigeria and Mexico enabled us to see how agrarian parents used the precocious arithmetical skills of their children in selling. Hausa girls as young as seven were sent out hawking goods in public places, and despite not having been to school, they had no trouble making change using the British pounds-shillings-pence system. In Mexico, we found girls the same age minding stalls in village plazas and on side streets in cities, earning money in the local community to be turned over to their parents. We couldn't help thinking of how much more supervision American middle-class parents consider necessary when they provide their children with lemonade to sell on the street in hot weather, allowing them to pocket the proceeds.

What Makes Children Precocious?

Examples of child precocity in different cultures range from the early work and responsibility training described in the previous chapter to self-reliance, talking, bilingualism, empathy, and selling. The data are not conclusive, but they suggest that one way of deciphering the parental agenda of a particular culture is to examine the behavior of the youngest children as reflecting their parents' priorities. Using the control they have over their infants and toddlers, parents *prime* them for participation in their community's cultural routines; priming shows us cultural priorities in action. But even if parental goals shape the precocious behavior of their infants, toddlers, or early school-age children, does that mean parental influence on child development is as long-lasting as has often been claimed? In the final chapter, we take up this question, considering how to think about it and what it might mean for parents.

~ 9 ~

Conclusions

THE PRACTICES OF America's recent parental generations have been described, analyzed, and criticized by social scientists, journalists, and parents since the 1990s. These observers claim that contemporary middle-class parents have greatly expanded the demands they put on themselves for parenting, even while they are busier than ever at work outside the home. They criticize the priorities of parents and their excessive, self-defeating practices, using terms like "helicopter parenting," "intensive parenting," "defensive parenting," "paranoid parenting," the "enslavement" of parents to their children, and finally, "the collapse of parenting."[1] Their practices are said to produce "entitled" and "disrespectful" children who may insult their parents and refuse to assume minimal responsibilities at home.

This literature includes systematic studies by sociologists (Sharon Hays, Annette Lareau, and Suzanne Bianchi), an anthropologist (Elinor Ochs), and a psychologist (Marie-Anne Suizzo).[2] A psychotherapist (Polly Young-Eisendrath) and a physician-psychologist (Leonard Sax) have also made informed analyses.[3]

There have been insightful accounts by journalists (Jennifer Senior and Pamela Druckerman) as well.[4] Their conclusions and critiques cannot be ignored. Their portraits of middle-class parenting are in stark contrast with those of the American working class, Parisians, and the rest of the world. Yet the child-rearing patterns they portray are rooted in a moral ideology of the loving egalitarian parent that has taken hold in the last thirty years.

Intensive Parenting in America

American middle-class parents, compared with parents elsewhere, feel burdened and anxious, not only about their children but about the effectiveness of their parenting. Ironically, the risk faced by our ancestors, of children dying before the age of five, has been reduced in the United States to a small fraction of what it was in 1900 or even 1950, owing primarily to public health and drug improvements, which require little of parents. Yet middle-class parents, facing this unprecedented assurance about their children's survival, seem more concerned about risks than ever. More educated and better informed than their forebears even a generation ago, they operate with a consciousness of the risks (quantified through published epidemiological findings) their children face, however low the probability of any harm coming to them. They have become susceptible to public scares about child molesters, playground accidents, and "harmful" vaccines and medicines.

In addition to being risk-averse, American middle-class parents impose burdens on themselves that seem unnecessary from a global perspective:

- Sleeplessness during the infant's first year, occasioned by putting the child in a separate room rather than in the parental bed, as discussed in Chapter 3.

- Presenting toddlers with choices about almost everything—
  food, activities, even where to cross the street—to avoid imposing parental authority as earlier generations of parents
  did. Parents want to be their children's *best friend*. Negotiating about which way to do something takes a lot more time
  and effort than following a script.

- Relieving school-age children of household responsibilities, as busy parents do for their children what children
  once did for themselves.

- Supplementing the school with tutoring by parents or
  lessons to which the child must be taken by the mother,
  regarded as essential for the child's development—what
  Annette Lareau calls "concerted cultivation." Although
  the *New York Times* headline "Is Your First Grader College
  Ready?" may be a joke, can parents resist the worry?[5]

At every stage from infancy to college, parenting has been
redefined to require more attention, thought, and energy from
parents, and young couples either embrace child-rearing as mas-
sively burdensome or reject it entirely to remain childless. Why?

Part of the answer is that many couples intend to have only
one or two children, and they are older and more affluent when
they start, so they are inclined to idealize their burdens as treasured contributions to their own and their children's lives. Moreover, many parents emphasize the competitiveness of the world
into which they're bringing their children, so they see the inten-
sity of their parenting as necessary as well as rewarding. And they
also tend to feel guilty that, given their commitments to jobs outside the home, they can't spend more time with their children.
Contemporary parents are convinced that parenting is not only a

major job itself but also a sacred trust requiring their investment of expertise, awareness of risks, and limitless time and effort. With this mind-set, they can hardly resist advice to do more for their children.

If you want to see how strange this can seem, follow an American mother named Pamela Druckerman to Paris, where she asks:

> Why is it . . . that in the hundreds of hours I've clocked at French playgrounds, I've never seen a child (except my own) throw a temper tantrum? Why don't my French friends ever need to rush off the phone because their kids are demanding something? Why haven't their living rooms been taken over by teepees and toy kitchens, the way ours has?
>
> When American families visit our home, the parents usually spend much of the visit refereeing their kids' spats, helping their toddlers do laps around the kitchen island, or getting down on the floor to build LEGO villages. There are always a few rounds of crying and consoling. When French friends visit, however, we grown-ups have coffee and the children play happily by themselves.[6]

When the psychologist Marie-Anne Suizzo conducted interviews with thirty-two mothers in Paris, she found them seeking to avoid becoming "enslaved" to their toddlers, who would otherwise become "child kings." French parents clearly have different goals and practices, though their culture is in many ways similar to that of Americans. What about the rest of the world?

Human Parenting

The varieties of human parenting examined in the foregoing chapters indicate that there is no single pattern of parenting provided by evolution or historical necessity. Parents' practices for infant care, training toddlers, and managing older children vary widely across the world and also over the generations in each particular place. These variations are no more predictable, nor even imaginable, from the infrastructure that makes them possible—the human genome, brain, and reproductive anatomy—than are the thousands of languages in the world made possible by our universal speech anatomy. Parental practices, like languages, cannot be discovered by theory or laboratory experiments; you must get out in the field to observe parents in context—more like Darwin than Pasteur. We now have observations of parenting from many, though not all, parts of the world, and the evidence is increasing in geographic coverage and developmental depth.

Premature attempts to build a general theory of human parenting have tended to oversimplify the evidence, ignore exceptions, and use fallacious analogies about adaptation or progress. At its extreme, the adaptationist approach reduces parenting to rational responses to current environmental pressures, leaving out the moral ideas passed on from previous generations. But it's the combination of that cultural legacy with environmental responsiveness that makes standards of parenting as complex—and surprising—as other aspects of culture. Regional traditions differentiate child-rearing in India from that in Thailand, for example, and parenting in East Africa (Kenya, Tanzania) from that of West Africa (Nigeria, Ivory Coast). There are also broad ecological conditions, such as family-based agriculture, that make agrarian peoples as a whole different from hunter-gatherers and modern societies, but we have shown that there are variations *within* each of these three categories. And each generation in a particular community has its own standards, much like the dialects of a language.

Furthermore, history shows that parenting is not a ladder-like progression with the most "developed" societies at the top.

On the contrary, parental practices in modern societies like our own, whatever their advantages, have problems aplenty. Nor is parenting simply a function of technological advance. Remember that synthetic milk formula, which was invented in 1867 and spread widely in Western countries, is now regarded as inferior to the breast-feeding practices of earlier times, which we share with other mammals. And caesarean surgery for childbirth is now overused in the United States, according to the World Health Organization and other medical authorities. Technological advances in reproduction and parenting have a tendency to become more popular than is good for us.

Pathways for the Development of Young Children

Parents provide culturally distinctive pathways for the development of their young children. The home, in its physical structure, social density, and daily routines, is the setting for care and early childhood learning and partly shapes what goes on there. Rather than improvising the care and training of offspring in that setting, parents follow a local, generation-specific code of parental conduct with scripts for the mother and other caregivers in guiding children's participation in domestic routines. Here are some examples:

- In the Indian joint family, there are not only more people sharing domestic resources than in middle-class America but also a much wider variety of adults and older children caring for, and in social contact with, every child.

- A similarly sharp contrast exists between the face-to-face communication—including mutual gaze, smiling, and talking—of Western middle-class parents with their babies and the skin-to-skin interactions of mother and infant in Africa and much of the agrarian world. On the one side, there is a mother seeking to excite her baby in an emotionally positive and highly verbal exchange across a physical distance, and on the other, a mother seeking to keep her child calm at all times. Such soothing may seem like "maternal deprivation" to us, but observations show that it not only doesn't harm the infant but actually prepares her for a future as a compliant and respectful toddler.

- In some of the Pacific Islands, parents play with their young toddlers, postponing demands for their compliance in tasks until they are five to six years old and (possibly) encountering tantrums during the transition.

- In many agrarian societies, learning can be gradual, as the growing child at home is able to observe others performing tasks—ranging from shucking corn and making tortillas to carrying water, caring for infants, and cultivating crops—before actually carrying them out. Parents may not teach but "guide" the child's participation in a production team.

As schooling spread in the transition to a modern or urban-industrial society, it changed the developmental pathways for agrarian children in terms of parents' goals for their children and the setting, curriculum, and relationships of the school. Urbanization, with parents employed outside the home, also changed the child's learning environment, toward school and away from the home. Yet parents who have recently come to the city may continue the agrarian pattern of training their children in responsibility, enlisting them in household tasks. The spread of schooling to rural communities around the world after 1950 blurred the divide between agrarian and modern societies in the predicament of parents and children. But it has not homogenized the ways in which parents train their young children, as the cross-cultural evidence on precocity shows.

Precocious Children and Parental Influence

The behavior of toddlers is highly responsive to their parents' priorities. In Chapter 8, we gave examples of young children showing proficiencies ranging from talking to compliance to agricultural tasks to infant care—at an age that would be considered precocious in a different culture—because their mothers had facilitated that early development. This seems to suggest powerful parental influence.

But does it last? There is reason to question long-term parental influence. In the early years—say, the first five years of a child's life—mothers and others in the home have an exceptional degree of control over the child's routine environment. But as the child gets older that control is likely to diminish as he or she is exposed to a wider world of environmental influences. Even some agrarian societies that have no schools and practice domestic food production also have initiation ceremonies, secret societies, or craft workshops that wrest control from parents over five- to ten-year-old children and provide indoctrination that might counter or dilute the early parental influence.

During adolescence, beginning at eleven to fourteen years of age, there are changes in the brain and the environment that could eradicate early parental influence. The influence of a social identity, in which the adolescent becomes attached to an ideal self-concept, might become more powerful than residues of early childhood experience. Our skepticism about long-term parental influence could only be dispelled by better evidence than we now have demonstrating that psychological dispositions shown in infancy and childhood are preserved into the mature years.

Resilience

Children change in their behavior and psychological development into their teen years, and whether they are harmed by early experiences remains a question. We have reviewed in this book many parental practices that are standard in one or more cultures around the world but that Western experts tell us are "traumatic," "abusive," or at least "adverse." Comparative observations lead us to question what an adverse experience is and what its consequences are likely to be. When mothers avoid looking at their infants and send them away to kin in the second year of life, are they inflicting trauma on their children? And if the children who had those experiences seem to be "normal" in adulthood to Western observers, what do we make of it?

Our conclusion is that, at the very least, the expectations generated by terms such as "adverse," "traumatic," and "abusive" have been exaggerated, and the resilience of children underestimated, in using Western psychiatry as a guide to human development in general. In other words, children are not as sensitive as the experts have told us, and parents in other cultures are not as insensitive to the welfare of their children as they might appear at first sight. We don't have all the evidence needed to settle the question of whether the parental practices described in this book inflict harm on adult mental health. But we do know that all too often when *their* practices depart from *our* standards, experts jump to the conclusion that the result will be psychopathology.

Trade-offs

Adults everywhere have multiple commitments. Even the German stay-at-home wife of old, the *Hausfrau* famously devoted to *Kinder, Küche, Kirche* (children, kitchen, church), had to balance child care with housework and church activities. In sub-Saharan Africa, as we have seen, women were often responsible for growing the household's food while bearing a dozen children, breast-feeding each one and supervising their work. They conformed to a routine established before they became mothers, not only for each day's activities but also for defined periods of intensive breast-feeding, followed by weaning and the toddler's involvement with a sibling group or "granny." In an agrarian society with such routines standardized, a mother had little choice in organizing the trade-offs involved. The routine was a constraint but also a *comfort* that prevented the anxiety of choice.

In our society, by contrast, mothers and fathers are on their own when it comes to balancing child care with work and other activities. There is no one else in the household to guide them, and furthermore, they define work and family as a set of personally motivated decisions, not formal obligations. Yet in the agrarian families of Africa, Mexico, and Nepal, where parenting is regarded as a matter of formal obligation, we were awed by the unambivalent dedication of mothers to the welfare of their children. These women were indeed the "ordinary devoted mothers" of which the British pediatrician D. W. Winnicott wrote many years ago, and those with sick or disabled children showed how devoted they were as they departed from their routines to tend them. Their formal parental roles proved at least as motivating as personally chosen goals are for parents in our own society.

Modern parents seek above all to optimize their children's life chances and exert a virtuous influence on their children's development. But as we have seen, the influence of parenting on child development has been grossly exaggerated in the mass media, which inflates its predictability beyond the evidence and underestimates the resilience of children and the likelihood of change in later childhood and adolescence. The time has come for American parents to reconsider the burdens they place on themselves for dubious ends.

In this reconsideration, parents need to look at evidence from other modern societies. In Japan, for example, parent-child co-sleeping is the norm, yet Japanese parents, in retaining that agrarian custom, can enjoy the benefits of being able to sleep through the night with their babies *without* endangering them. In fact, the Japanese rates of infant mortality and SIDS are much lower than ours. Chinese mothers are as concerned with their children's futures as we are, but they freely criticize their toddlers and encourage a level of compliance that permits them to be far less labor-intensive in their parenting than the negotiating American parent who offers choices to the youngest of toddlers.

These are a few examples from the evidence reviewed in this book. Once American parents free themselves from the expert warnings that any deviations from current American practices will constitute trauma, abuse, or adversity for their children's development—warnings that we have shown are largely groundless—then it will be possible to learn from other cultures and reduce parental burdens to a more sensible level.

Acknowledgments

We have many to thank, beginning with our literary agent Erika Storella and her colleagues at the Gernert Company, who worked with us from 2011 on each phase of the project. Helping mightily to get us going was the research assistance of Julia Hayden, who explored the cross-cultural literature on child development beyond our own areas of expertise. Once we began writing, the feedback from our colleagues Paul Harris, Heidi Keller, Jerome Kagan, and Christine Gross-Loh was invaluable, and we are also indebted to John Demos and his Yale colleague Keith Wrightson for guiding us to the literature on that most exotic of cultures, preindustrial England. Janet Steins and Susan Gilman, librarians at Tozzer Library, Harvard, helped us find photographs in the archives. We thank Ben Adams, our editor at PublicAffairs, for his helpful comments as a parent as well as editor, and his expert guidance through the publication process. We also thank Jane Bretherton, Anna Winger, Susan Aird, Judy Ellenzweig, Sheila Hoadley, Sally Webster, and Chris Dadian for their interest in, and support for, the project over the last five years. And finally, we are grateful for a fellowship on the anthropology of parenting from the John Simon Guggenheim Memorial Foundation in 2004–2005, which provided support when this project, and our first grandchild, were in their infancy. We take sole responsibility for the final product.

Notes

Introduction. We the Parents: A Worldwide Perspective

1. The Hausa number at least 20 million and live not only in northern Nigeria but also in Niger and other West African countries.

2. The Hausa we worked with in a small town of Katsina province in northwestern Nigeria call themselves Fulani, or Hausa-Fulani, to emphasize their descent from the Fulani who conquered their Hausa ancestors in the early nineteenth century under the Fulani leader Usman dan Fodio.

3. Margaret Mead, *Growing Up in New Guinea* (New York: William Morrow, 1930).

4. Joseph Henrich, Steven J. Heine, and Ara Norenzayan. "The Weirdest People in the World?" *Behavioral and Brain Sciences* 33 (2010): 1–23.

5. Robert A. LeVine, Suzanne Dixon, Sarah LeVine, Amy Richman, P. Herbert Leiderman, and T. Berry Brazelton, *Child Care and Culture: Lessons from Africa* (New York: Cambridge University Press, 1994), 47. See Alma Gottlieb, *The Afterlife Is Where We Come From* (Chicago: University of Chicago Press, 2007), for a fuller account of a West African community that resembles the Yoruba.

6. Shusuke Kobayashi, "Japanese Mother-Child Relationships: Skill Acquisition Before the Preschool Years," in *Japanese Frames of Mind: Cultural Perspectives on Human Development*, edited by Hidetada Shimizu and Robert A. LeVine (New York: Cambridge University Press, 2001), 111–140; Heidi Fung, "Becoming a Moral Child: The Socialization of Shame Among Young Chinese Children," *Ethos* 27 (1999): 180–209; Peggy J. Miller, Todd L. Sandel, Chung-Hui Liang, and Heidi Fung, "Narrating Transgressions in Longwood: The Discourses, Meanings, and Paradoxes of an American Socializing Practice," *Ethos* 29, no. 2 (2001): 159–186.

7. Alan Macfarlane, *The Origins of English Individualism: The Family, Property and Social Transition* (New York: Cambridge University Press, 1978), 174–175.

8. Annette Lareau, *Unequal Childhoods: Class, Race and Family Life* (Berkeley: University of California Press, 2003); Jennifer Senior, *All Joy and No Fun: The Paradox of Modern Parenthood* (New York: Ecco, 2014).

Chapter 1. Parent-Blaming in America

1. Horace Mann, *Report of an Educational Tour in Germany and Parts of Great Britain and Ireland* (London: Simpkin, Marshall & Co., 1846).

2. L. Emmett Holt, *The Care and Feeding of Children: A Catechism for the Use of Mothers and Children's Nurses,* 7th ed. (New York: D. Appleton & Co., 1914).

3. Ibid., 163, 170, 174, and 176.

4. Specifically, *Ladies' Home Journal, Woman's Home Companion,* and *Good Housekeeping,* which are analyzed by Celia B. Stendler in "Sixty Years of Child Training Practices: Revolution in the Nursery," *Journal of Pediatrics* 36 (1950): 122–134.

5. For example, the British pediatrician Winifred de Kok, in *Guiding Your Child Through the Formative Years: From Birth to the Age of Five* (New York: Emerson Books, 1935), 109.

6. Stendler, "Sixty Years of Child Training Practices," 128.

7. Paul Starr, *The Social Transformation of American Medicine* (New York: Basic Books, 1982).

8. Ibid.

9. Ann Hulbert, *Raising America: Experts, Parents, and a Century of Advice About Children* (New York: Random House, 2003), 11.

10. John B. Watson, *Psychological Care of Infant and Child* (New York: W. W. Norton, 1928).

11. Ibid., 80.

12. Stendler, "Sixty Years of Child Training Practices," 122.

13. Urie Bronfenbrenner, "Socialization and Social Class Through Time and Space," in *Readings in Social Psychology,* 3rd ed., edited by Eleanor E. Maccoby, Theodore M. Newcomb, and Eugene L. Hartley (New York: Holt, Rinehart & Winston, 1958), 400–425.

14. Stendler, "Sixty Years of Child Training Practices," 132.

15. Benjamin Spock, *The Common Sense Book of Baby and Child Care* (New York: Duell, Sloan and Pearce, 1946), 3.

16. Ibid., 47.

17. Sigmund Freud, "Three Essays on the Theory of Sexuality" (1905), in *The Standard Edition of the Complete Psychological Works of Sigmund Freud,* vol. 7, edited by James Strachey (London: Hogarth Press, 1953), 125–243.

18. Sigmund Freud, "The Ego and the Id" (1923), in *The Standard Edition of the Complete Psychological Works of Sigmund Freud,* vol. 19, edited by James Strachey (London: Hogarth Press, 1961), 12–66.

19. Karen Horney, *The Neurotic Personality of Our Time* (New York: W. W. Norton, 1937); Karen Horney, *New Ways in Psychoanalysis* (New York: W. W. Norton, 1939).

20. Karen Horney, *Neurosis and Human Growth* (New York: W. W. Norton, 1950), 18.

21. An earlier version of the book had been published in 1951 as *Maternal Care and Mental Health,* a report commissioned by the World Health Organization.

22. See the recent cross-cultural critiques: Hiltrud Otto and Heidi Keller, eds., *Different Faces of Attachment: Cultural Variations on a Universal Human Need* (Cambridge: Cambridge University Press, 2014); Naomi Quinn and Jeanette Mageo, eds., *Attachment Reconsidered: Cultural Perspectives on a Western Theory* (New York: Palgrave Macmillan, 2013).

23. Mary D. Salter Ainsworth, Mary C. Blehar, Everett Waters, and Sally N. Wall, *Patterns of Attachment: A Psychological Study of the Strange Situation* (Hillsdale, NJ: Erlbaum, 1978).

24. Harry Stack Sullivan, *Conceptions of Modern Psychiatry* (New York: W. W. Norton, 1940). See also Helen Swick Perry, *Psychiatrist of America: The Life of Harry Stack Sullivan* (Cambridge, MA: Harvard University Press, 1982).

25. Frieda Fromm-Reichmann, "Notes on the Development of Treatment of Schizophrenics by Psychoanalytic Psychotherapy," *Psychiatry* 11 (1948): 263–273.

26. Gregory Bateson, Don D. Jackson, Jay Haley, and John Weakland. "Toward a Theory of Schizophrenia," *Behavioral Science* 1 (1956): 251–264.

27. David Lipset, *Gregory Bateson: The Legacy of a Scientist* (Englewood Cliffs, NJ: Prentice-Hall, 1980), 206.

28. Anne Harrington, "The Fall of the Schizophrenogenic Mother," *The Lancet* 379 (April 7, 2012): 1292–1293.

29. See, for example, R. D. Laing, *The Politics of the Family, and Other Essays* (Harmondsworth, UK: Penguin, 1976).

30. Harrington, "The Fall of the Schizophrenogenic Mother," 1293.

31. Ibid.

32. Bruno Bettelheim, *The Empty Fortress: Infantile Autism and the Birth of the Self* (New York: Free Press, 1967), 125.

33. Bruno Bettelheim, *Love Is Not Enough* (Glencoe, IL: Free Press, 1950).

34. Ibid., 16–17.

35. Ibid., 7.

36. NICHD Early Child Care Research Network, "The Effects of Infant Child Care on Infant-Mother Attachment Security: Results of the NICHD Study of Early Child Care," *Child Development* 68, no. 5 (1997): 860–879.

37. Robert J. Trotter, "Human Behavior: Do Animals Have the Answer?" *Science News* 105 (1974): 279.

38. NICHD Early Child Care Research Network, "The Effects of Infant Child Care on Infant-Mother Attachment Security," 875.

39. Marga Vicedo, *The Nature and Nurture of Love: From Imprinting to Attachment in Cold War America* (Chicago: University of Chicago Press, 2013).

40. Jerome Kagan, *The Human Spark: The Science of Human Development* (New York: Basic Books, 2013), 129, 156.

Chapter 2. Expecting: Pregnancy and Birth

1. Sarah LeVine, *Mothers and Wives: Gusii Women of East Africa* (Chicago: University of Chicago Press, 1979).

2. Gusii women did not imbibe alcoholic beverages in the 1950s, even while they served millet-beer to men, who became drunk. The one exception was a woman who was stigmatized in the community; people talked behind her back. But when Bob returned seventeen years later, in 1974, many women were brewing beer (or even distilling spirits) to add to the family income, and women were no longer stigmatized for drinking.

3. Gananath Obeyesekere, "Pregnancy Cravings (Dola-Duka) in Relation to Social Structure and Personality in a Sinhalese Village," *American Anthropologist* 65 (1963): 323–342.

4. Ruth Freed and Stanley Freed, "Rites of Passage in Shanti Nagar," *Anthropological Papers of the American Museum of Natural History* 56 (1980): 351–353.

5. Kim Gutschow, *Being a Buddhist Nun: The Struggle for Enlightenment in the Himalayas* (Cambridge, MA: Harvard University Press, 2004), 209–210.

6. Kim Gutschow, "From Home to Hospital: The Extension of Obstetrics in Ladakh," in *Medicine Between Science and Religion: Explorations on Tibetan Grounds,* edited by Vincanne Adams, Mona Schrempf, and Sienna Craig (London: Berghahn Press, 2011), 204.

7. Lynn Bennett, *Dangerous Wives and Sacred Sisters: Social and Symbolic Roles of High-Caste Women in Nepal* (New York: Columbia University Press, 1983).

8. Barbara Rogoff, *Developing Destinies: A Mayan Wife and Town* (New York: Oxford University Press, 2011).

9. Marjorie Shostak, *Nisa: The Life and Words of a !Kung Woman* (Cambridge, MA: Harvard University Press, 1981); Megan Biesele, "An Ideal of Unassisted Birth: Hunting, Healing, and Transformation Among the Kalahari Ju/'hoansi," in *Childbirth and Authoritative Knowledge: Cross-Cultural Perspectives*, edited by Robbie Davis-Floyd and Carolyn Sargent (Berkeley: University of California Press, 1997).

10. Melvin J. Konner, "Aspects of the Developmental Ethology of a Foraging People," in *Ethological Studies of Child Behavior*, edited by Nicholas Blurton-Jones (Cambridge: Cambridge University Press, 1972), 288.

11. The leaves on the placenta are called *emesabakwa* and are also used in initiation ceremonies. The word for "placenta" in the Gusii language is *omogoye*, and it also denotes the bark strips that held together Gusii house frames before the advent of nails. Thus, the placenta with the leaves metaphorically represents a house that continues to protect the womb.

12. Rogoff, *Developing Destinies*; Brigitte Jordan, *Birth in Four Cultures: A Crosscultural Investigation of Childbirth in Yucatan, Holland, Sweden, and the United States*, 4th ed. (Long Grove, IL: Waveland Press, 1993).

13. Sarah Hrdy, *Mother Nature: A History of Mothers, Infants, and Natural Selection* (New York: Pantheon, 1999), 297–317; David Kertzer, *Sacrificed for Honor: Italian Infant Abandonment and the Politics of Reproductive Control* (Boston: Beacon Press, 1993).

14. Francesco Cardini and Huang Weixin, "Moxibustion for Correction of Breech Presentation: A Randomized Controlled Trial," *Journal of the American Medical Association* 280 (1998): 1580–1584.

Chapter 3. Infant Care:
A World of Questions . . . and Some Answers

1. John Bowlby, *Child Care and the Growth of Love* (Harmondsworth, UK: Penguin, 1953), 50, 66.

2. United Nations Department of Economic and Social Affairs, Population Division, *World Population Prospects: The 2012 Revision: Volume 1, Highlights and Advance Tables*.

3. United Nations Secretary-General's Office, *The Millennium Goals Report 2015*, http://www.un.org/millenniumgoals/2015_MDG_Report/pdf/MDG%202015%20rev%20(July%201).pdf.

4. Adam Fifield, *A Mighty Purpose: How Jim Grant Sold the World on Saving Its Children* (New York: Other Press, 2015).

5. John Whiting, "Environmental Constraints on Infant Care Practices," in *Culture and Human Development: The Selected Papers of John Whiting,* edited by Eleanor C. Chasdi (New York: Cambridge University Press, 1993), 134.

6. Wayne Dennis, *The Hopi Child* (New York: Wiley, 1940).

7. James S. Chisholm, *Navajo Infancy: An Ethological Study of Child Development* (Hawthorne, NY: Aldine, 1983).

8. Robert S. Marvin, Thomas L. VanDevender, Margaret I. Iwanaga, Sarah LeVine, and Robert A. LeVine, "Infant-Caregiver Attachment Among the Hausa of Nigeria," in *Ecological Factors in Human Development,* edited by Harry McGurk (Amsterdam: North-Holland Publishing, 1977).

9. Robert R. Sears, Eleanor E. Maccoby, and Harry Levin, *Patterns of Child Rearing* (New York: Harper & Row, 1957), 73.

10. John Newson and Elizabeth Newson, *Patterns of Infant Care in an Urban Community* (Harmondsworth, UK: Penguin Books, 1963), 32.

11. Jill Lepore, "Baby Food," *The New Yorker,* January 19, 2009.

12. Harvey Levenstein, "'Best for Babies' or 'Preventable Infanticide'? The Controversy over Artificial Feeding of Infants in America, 1880–1920," *Journal of American History* 70 (1983): 75–94.

13. US Department of Health and Human Services, Centers for Disease Control and Prevention (CDC), "Breastfeeding Report Card—United States, 2011," http://www.cdc.gov/breastfeeding/pdf/2011breastfeedingreportcard.pdf.

14. Lepore's article "Baby Food," on breast pumps, details the lengths to which contemporary American working mothers go to provide their own breast milk to their children even when they cannot nurse them.

15. In Nigeria and other parts of Africa, it had become customary by the 1950s to feed children after weaning a diet made up almost entirely of cassava, a South American root crop low in protein; this practice led to a high prevalence of protein-calorie malnutrition among two- to four-year-old children.

16. William Caudill and David Plath, "Who Sleeps by Whom? Parent-Child Involvement in Urban Japanese Families," *Psychiatry* 29 (1966): 344–366; Christine Gross-Loh, *Parenting Without Borders: Surprising Lessons Parents Around the World Can Teach Us* (New York: Avery, 2013), 26.

17. University of Notre Dame, Mother-Baby Behavioral Sleep Laboratory, cosleeping.nd.edu.

18. Task Force on Sudden Infant Death Syndrome, "SIDS and Other Sleep-Related Infant Deaths: Expansion of Recommendations for a Safe Infant Sleeping Environment," *Pediatrics* 128 (2011): e1341–e1367.

19. Ibid., e1350.

20. Sigmund Freud, "From the History of an Infantile Neurosis" (1918), in *The Standard Edition of the Complete Psychological Works of Sigmund Freud*, vol. 17, edited by James Strachey (London: Hogarth Press, 1955), 3–122. This is the case account of a patient known as the "Wolf-man" in which Freud first attributed a patient's neurosis to the memory of witnessing parental intercourse.

21. Paul Okami, "Childhood Exposure to Parental Nudity, Parent-Child Co-sleeping, and 'Primal Scenes': A Review of Clinical Opinion and Empirical Evidence," *Journal of Sex Research* 32 (1995): 51–64.

22. Paul Okami, "Early Childhood Exposure to Parental Nudity and Scenes of Parental Sexuality ('Primal Scenes'): An 18-Year Longitudinal Study of Outcome," *Archives of Sexual Behavior* 27 (1998): 361–384.

23. See Chapter 9 for a fuller account. See also Margaret Mahler, Fred Pine, and Anni Bergmann, *The Psychological Birth of the Human Infant* (New York: Basic Books, 1975).

24. Caudill and Plath, "Who Sleeps by Whom?"

25. Gross-Loh, *Parenting Without Borders*, 26–27.

26. James McKenna and Lee Gettler, "There Is No Such Thing as Infant Sleep, There Is No Such Thing as Breast-feeding, There Is Only Breast-sleeping," *Acta Paediatrica* 105 (2016): 17–21.

27. Richard A. Shweder, Lene Jensen, and William Goldstein, "Who Sleeps by Whom Revisited: A Method for Extracting the Moral 'Goods' Implicit in Praxis," in *Cultural Practices as Context for Development*, vol. 67, *New Directions for Child Development*, edited by Jacqueline Goodnow, Peggy Miller, and Frank Kessel (San Francisco: Jossey-Bass, 1995).

Chapter 4. Mother and Infant: Face-to-Face or Skin-to-Skin?

1. Walter Goldschmidt, "Absent Eyes and Idle Hands: Socialization for Low Affect Among the Sebei," in *Socialization as Cultural Communication: Development of a Theme in the Work of Margaret Mead*, edited by Theodore Schwartz (Berkeley: University of California Press, 1976); Relindis Yovsi, Joscha Kartner, Heidi Keller, and A. Lohaus, "Maternal Interactional Quality in Two Cultural Environments," *Journal of Cross-Cultural Psychology* 40 (2009): 701–707.

2. Heidi Keller, *Cultures of Infancy* (Mahwah, NJ: LEA, 2007), 96.

3. Joscha Kartner, Heidi Keller, and Relindis Yovsi, "Mother-Infant Interaction During the First 3 Months: The Emergence of Culture-Specific Contingency Patterns," *Child Development* 81 (2010): 540–554.

4. Robert A. LeVine, Suzanne Dixon, Sarah LeVine, Amy Richman, P. Herbert Leiderman, and T. Berry Brazelton, *Child Care and Culture: Lessons from Africa* (New York: Cambridge University Press, 1994).

5. Robert A. LeVine and Barbara B. Lloyd, *Nyansongo: A Gusii Community in Kenya* (New York: Wiley, 1966), 124.

6. Amy Richman, Patrice M. Miller, and Robert A. LeVine, "Cultural and Educational Variations in Maternal Responsiveness," *Developmental Psychology* 28 (1992): 614–621.

7. D. W. Winnicott, *The Child and the Family: First Relationships* (London: Tavistock, 1957).

8. Melvin Konner, "Aspects of the Developmental Ethology of a Foraging People," in *Ethological Studies of Child Behavior,* edited by Nicholas Blurton-Jones (Cambridge: Cambridge University Press, 1972), 292, 294.

9. Marjorie Shostak, *Nisa: The Life and Words of a !Kung Woman* (Cambridge, MA: Harvard University Press, 1981), 41.

10. Barry Hewlett, *Intimate Fathers: The Nature and Context of Aka Pygmy Paternal Infant Care* (Ann Arbor: University of Michigan Press, 1991), 32.

11. Ibid., 94.

12. Alma Gottlieb, *The Afterlife Is Where We Come From: The Culture of Infancy in West Africa* (Chicago: University of Chicago Press, 2004), 102.

13. Robert A. LeVine, Sarah LeVine, Beatrice Schnell-Anzola, Meredith Rowe, and Emily Dexter, *Literacy and Mothering: How Women's Schooling Changes the Lives of the World's Children* (New York: Oxford University Press, 2012), 14.

14. Robert A. LeVine, "Challenging Expert Knowledge: Findings from an African Study of Infant Care and Development," in *Childhood and Adolescence: Cross-Cultural Perspectives and Applications,* edited by Uwe Gielen and Jaipaul Roopnarine (Westport, CT: Praeger, 2004), 149–165.

15. See, for example, Jerome Kagan, *The Human Spark: The Science of Human Development* (New York: Basic Books, 2013), 125–156.

16. Heidi Keller, personal communication with the authors, 2005.

17. Heinz Kohut, *The Analysis of the Self* (New York: International Universities Press, 1971), 123–124.

18. Heidi Keller, *Cultures of Infancy* (Mahwah, NJ: Erlbaum, 2007).

19. Suzanne Dixon, Robert A. LeVine, Amy Richman, and T. Berry Brazelton, "Mother-Child Interaction Around a Teaching Task," *Child Development* 55 (1984): 1252–1264.

20. LeVine et al., *Child Care and Culture*, 216.

21. Keller, *Cultures of Infancy.*

22. Tiffany Field, "Touch for Socio-emotional and Physical Well-being: A Review," *Developmental Review* 30 (2010): 367–383.

Chapter 5. Sharing Child Care: Mom Is Not Enough

1. The Gusii have a proverb: "Someone else's child is like cold mucus" (i.e., disgusting); see Robert A. LeVine and Barbara Lloyd, *Nyansongo: A Gusii Community in Kenya* (New York: Wiley, 1966), 120.

2. Edward Z. Tronick, Gilda Morelli, and Steve Winn, "Multiple Caretaking of Efe (Pygmy) Infants," *American Anthropologist* 89 (1987): 96–106.

3. Alma Gottlieb, *The Afterlife Is Where We Come From: The Culture of Infancy in West Africa* (Chicago: University of Chicago Press, 2004), 202–204.

4. Dinesh Sharma and Robert A. LeVine, "Child Care in India: A Comparative Developmental View of Infant Social Environments," in *Socioemotional Development Across Cultures,* edited by Dinesh Sharma and Kurt Fischer, New Directions for Child Development 81 (San Francisco: Jossey-Bass, 1998), 55.

5. Ruth S. Freed and Stanley A. Freed, "Enculturation and Education in Shanti Nagar" (monograph), *Anthropological Papers of the American Museum of Natural History* 57, part 2 (1981): 66, 71, 73.

6. Susan C. Seymour, *Women, Family, and Child Care in India: A World in Transition* (New York: Cambridge University Press, 1999), 81.

7. Ibid., 74.

8. Birgitt Röttger-Rössler, "Bonding and Belonging Beyond WEIRD Worlds: Re-thinking Attachment Theory on the Basis of Cross-cultural Anthropological Data," in *Different Faces of Attachment: Cultural Variations on a Universal Human Need,* edited by Hiltrud Otto and Heidi Keller (Cambridge: Cambridge University Press, 2014), 141–168.

9. Melvin J. Konner, "Relations Among Infants and Juveniles in Comparative Perspective," in *Friendship and Peer Relations,* edited by Michael Lewis and Leonard A. Rosenblum (New York: Wiley, 1975), 99–129.

10. Barry Hewlett, *Intimate Fathers: The Nature and Context of Aka Pygmy Paternal Infant Care* (Ann Arbor: University of Michigan Press, 1991).

11. Bronislaw Malinowski, *The Sexual Life of Savages in North-Western Melanesia* (London: George Routledge & Sons, 1929), 14–15.

12. The childless women suffered from secondary infertility due to gonorrhea. See Ulla Larsen, "A Comparative Study of the Levels and the Differentials of Sterility in Cameroon, Kenya, and Sudan," in *Reproduction and Social Organization in Sub-Saharan Africa*, edited by Ron J. Lesthaeghe (Berkeley: University of California Press, 1989).

13. Caroline Bledsoe and Uche Isiugo-Abanihe, "Strategies of Child-Fosterage Among Mende Grannies in Sierra Leone," in Lesthaeghe, *Reproduction and Social Organization in Sub-Saharan Africa*.

14. Vern Carroll, ed., *Adoption in Eastern Oceania* (Honolulu: University of Hawaii Press, 1970); Mary Martini and John Kirkpatrick, "Parenting in Polynesia: A View from the Marquesas," in *Parent-Child Socialization in Diverse Cultures*, edited by Jaipaul L. Roopnarine and Bruce Carter, vol. 5 of *Annual Advances in Applied Developmental Psychology* (Norwood, NJ: Ablex, 1992).

Chapter 6. Training Toddlers:
Talking, Toileting, Tantrums, and Tasks

1. Jean Briggs, *Inuit Morality Play: The Emotional Education of a Three-Year-Old* (New Haven, CT: Yale University Press, 1998), 5.

2. Ibid., 6.

3. Barbara Rogoff, Jayanthi Mistry, Artin Göncü, Christine Mosier, Pablo Chavajay, and Shirley Brice Health, "Guided Participation in Cultural Activity by Toddlers and Caregivers," *Monographs of the Society for Research in Child Development* 58, serial no. 236 (1993).

4. Inge Bolin, *Growing Up in a Culture of Respect* (Austin: University of Texas Press, 2006), 73.

5. These are the upper-caste Brahmin-Chetris (or Parbatiyas) of Nepal. They speak Nepali as their native language, are more than 40 percent of the national population, and resemble the Hindus of northern India in their culture.

6. Bambi Schieffelin and Elinor Ochs, eds., *Language Socialization Across Cultures* (Cambridge: Cambridge University Press, 1986).

7. Sara Harkness and Charles M. Super, "Why African Children Are So Hard to Test," in *Issues in Cross-Cultural Research*, edited by Leonard Loeb Adler (New York: New York Academy of Sciences, 1977), 326–331.

8. Judith R. Johnston and M.-Y. Anita Wong, "Cultural Difference in Beliefs and Practices Concerning Talk to Children," *Journal of Speech, Language, and Hearing Research* 45 (2002): 916–926.

9. Joseph Tobin, Yeh Hsueh, and Mayumi Karasawa, *Preschool in Three Cultures Revisited: China, Japan, and the United States* (Chicago: University of Chicago Press, 2009).

10. Ibid., 65.

11. Ibid.

12. Ibid., 65, note 90.

13. Miller et al., "Narrating Transgressions in Longwood."

14. Bambi Schieffelin, *The Give and Take of Everyday Life: Language Socialization of Kaluli Children* (Cambridge: Cambridge University Press, 1990), 112–135.

15. Patricia M. Clancy, "The Socialization of Affect in Japanese Mother-Child Conversation," *Journal of Pragmatics* 31 (1999): 1397–1421.

16. John A. Martin, David R. King, Eleanor E. Maccoby, and Carol Nagy Jacklin, "Secular Trends and Individual Differences in Toilet-Training Progress," *Journal of Pediatric Psychology* 9 (1984): 457–467.

17. Newson and Newson, *Patterns of Infant Care in an Urban Community*, 118.

18. Marian R. Yarrow, John D. Campbell, and Roger V. Burton, *Child Rearing: An Inquiry into Research and Methods* (San Francisco: Jossey-Bass, 1968).

19. T. Berry Brazelton, "A Child-Oriented Approach to Toilet Training," *Pediatrics* 29 (1962): 579–588.

20. Mei-Ling Hopgood, *How Eskimos Keep Their Babies Warm and Other Adventures in Parenting* (Chapel Hill, NC: Algonquin Books, 2012); Freed and Freed, "Enculturation and Education in Shanti Nagar," 57.

21. Freed and Freed, 63.

22. Seymour, *Women, Family and Child Care in India,* 83.

23. Michael Potegal, Michael R. Kosorok, and Richard J. Davidson, "Temper Tantrums in Young Children: 2. Tantrum Duration and Temporal Organization," *Journal of Developmental and Behavioral Pediatrics* 24 (2003): 148. See also Michael Potegal, Michael R. Kosorok, and Richard J. Davidson, "Temper Tantrums in Young Children: 1. Behavioral Composition," *Journal of Developmental and Behavioral Pediatrics* 24 (2003): 140–147.

24. Jean Walker MacFarlane, Lucile Allen, and Marjorie P. Honzik, *A Developmental Study of the Behavior Problems of Normal Children Between 21 Months and 14 Years* (Berkeley: University of California Press, 1954).

See also Florence L. Goodenough, *Anger in Young Children* (Minneapolis: University of Minnesota Press, 1931).

25. John Newson and Elizabeth Newson, *Four Years Old in an Urban Community* (London: George Allen & Unwin, 1968), 448.

26. Ibid., 448, 450.

27. Allen Johnson, *Families of the Forest: Matsigenka Indians of the Peruvian Amazon* (Berkeley: University of California Press, 2003), 106–108.

28. Ibid., 108–109.

29. Elinor Ochs and Carolina Izquierdo, "Responsibility in Childhood: Three Developmental Trajectories," *Ethos* 37 (2009): 394.

30. Ibid., 395–396.

31. Homer G. Barnett, *Being a Palauan* (New York: Henry Holt, 1960), 4–5.

32. Ibid., 6.

33. Ibid., 7.

34. Harald Broch, *Growing Up Agreeably: Bonerate Childhood Observed* (Honolulu: University of Hawaii Press, 1990); Douglas Hollan and Jane Wellenkamp, *The Thread of Life: Toraja Reflections on the Life Cycle* (Honolulu: University of Hawaii Press, 1996).

35. Martini and Kirkpatrick, "Parenting in Polynesia"; Raymond Firth, *We the Tikopia* (1936; reprint edition, Boston: Beacon Press, 1963), 137–138.

36. Margaret Mead, *Coming of Age in Samoa* (New York: William Morrow, 1928).

37. Jeanette M. Mageo, "Toward a Cultural Psychodynamics of Attachment: Samoa and US Comparisons," in *Attachment Reconsidered: Cultural Perspectives on a Western Theory,* edited by Naomi Quinn and Jeanette M. Mageo (New York: Palgrave Macmillan, 2013), 199.

38. Malinowski, *The Sexual Life of Savages,* 19.

39. Mead, *Growing Up in New Guinea,* 38, 82.

40. Karen Watson-Gegeo, "Fantasy and Reality: The Dialectic of Work and Play in Kwara'ae Children's Lives," *Ethos* 29 (2001): 138–158.

Chapter 7. Childhood: School, Responsibility, and Control

1. Arnold Sameroff and Marshall Haith, eds., *The Five to Seven Year Shift: The Age of Reason and Responsibility* (Chicago: University of Chicago Press, 1996).

2. Barbara Rogoff, *Apprenticeship in Thinking: Cognitive Development in Social Context* (New York: Oxford University Press, 1990); Jean Lave

and Etienne Wenger, *Situated Learning: Legitimate Peripheral Participation* (Cambridge: Cambridge University Press, 1991).

3. Suzanne Gaskins, "Children's Daily Activities in a Mayan Village: A Culturally Grounded Description," *Cross-Cultural Research* 34 (2000): 375–389.

4. On Guatemala, see Rogoff, *Apprenticeship in Thinking,* 128. The psychologist-anthropologist Ashley Maynard was taught to make tortillas by Mayan women in Chiapas, Mexico (Zinacantán, the village of Nabenchauk); see Ashley Maynard, "Cultural Teaching: The Development of Teaching Skills in Maya Sibling Interactions," *Child Development* 73 (2002): 969–982. On the lowlands of Yucatán, see Suzanne Gaskins and Ruth Paradise, "Learning Through Observation in Daily Life," in *The Anthropology of Learning in Childhood,* edited by David Lancy, John Bock, and Suzanne Gaskins (Lanham, MD: Alta Mira Press, 2010), 85–118.

5. Ruth Paradise and Barbara Rogoff, "Side by Side: Learning by Observing and Pitching In," *Ethos* 37 (2009): 102–138.

6. David Lancy, *The Anthropology of Childhood: Cherubs, Chattel, Changelings* (New York: Cambridge University Press, 2008), 234–236.

7. David Lancy, *Playing on the Mother-Ground: Cultural Routines for Children's Development* (New York: Guilford Press, 1996), 145–146.

8. Children's learning in everyday contexts in agrarian societies has been intensively observed and instructively analyzed by Patricia Marks Greenfield, *Weaving Generations Together: Evolving Creativity in the Maya of Chiapas* (Santa Fe, NM: School of America Press, 2004), as well as by Barbara Rogoff, Ashley Maynard, and the contributors to Lancy et al., *The Anthropology of Learning in Childhood.*

9. Seymour, *Women, Family, and Child Care in India.*

10. Susan Seymour, "Expressions of Responsibility Among Indian Children: Some Precursors of Adult Status and Sex Roles," *Ethos* 16 (1988): 355–370.

11. Myron Weiner, *The Child and the State in India: Child Labor and Education Policy in Comparative Perspective* (Princeton, NJ: Princeton University Press, 1991), 33.

12. Macfarlane, *The Origins of English Individualism,* 195–196.

13. Ann Kussmaul, *Servants in Husbandry in Early Modern England* (Cambridge: Cambridge University Press, 1981), 76.

14. Ralph A. Houlbrooke, *The English Family, 1450–1700* (London: Longman Group Ltd., 1984), 153–154.

15. Steven Mintz, *Huck's Raft: A History of American Childhood* (Cambridge, MA: Harvard University Press, 2004), 150.

16. Lancy, *Playing on the Mother-Ground*, 95–143.

17. Charles Stafford, *The Roads of Chinese Childhood: Learning and Identification in Angang* (New York: Cambridge University Press, 1995), 56–57.

18. Jin Li, *Cultural Foundations of Learning: East and West* (New York: Cambridge University Press, 2012).

19. Ibid., 50.

20. Murray A. Straus, "Corporal Punishment," in *The Child: An Encyclopedic Companion,* edited by Richard A. Shweder (Chicago: University of Chicago Press, 2009), 214.

21. "British End School Caning," *New York Times,* July 24, 1986.

22. Jomo Kenyatta, *Facing Mount Kenya* (1938; reprint, New York: Vintage Books, 1962).

Chapter 8. Precocious Children:
Cultural Priming by Parents and Others

1. Pamela Druckerman, *Bringing Up Bébé* (New York: Penguin Press, 2012); Karen LeBillon, *French Kids Eat Everything* (New York: Harper Collins, 2012).

2. Ainsworth et al., *Patterns of Attachment.*

3. Karin Grossmann, Klaus E. Grossmann, Gottfried Spangler, Gerhard Suess, and Lothar Unzner, "Maternal Sensitivity and Newborns' Orientation Responses as Related to Quality of Attachment in Northern Germany," in *Growing Points of Attachment: Theory and Research,* edited by Inge Bretherton and Everett Waters, *Monographs of the Society for Research in Child Development* (Chicago: University of Chicago Press) 50, nos. 1–2 (1985), 253, 255.

4. Ibid., 236.

5. Karin Grossmann and Klaus Grossmann, "Newborn Behavior, the Quality of Early Parenting, and Later Toddler-Parent Relationships in a Group of German Infants," in *The Cultural Context of Infancy,* vol. 2, edited by J. Kevin Nugent, Barry M. Lester, and T. Berry Brazelton (Norwood, NJ: Ablex, 1991), 30.

6. Grossmann et al., "Maternal Sensitivity and Newborns' Orientation Responses," 246, table 1.

7. Karin Grossmann, Klaus E. Grossmann, Heinz Kindler, and Peter Zimmermann, "A Wider View of Attachment and Exploration: The Influ-

ence of Mothers and Fathers on the Development of Psychological Security from Infancy to Young Adulthood," in *Handbook of Attachment,* edited by Jude Cassidy and Philip R. Shaver (New York: Guilford Press, 2008), 857–879; Thomas S. Weisner, "Attachment as a Cultural and Ecological Problem with Pluralistic Solutions," *Human Development* 48 (2005): 89–94.

8. Ochs and Izquierdo, "Responsibility in Childhood."

9. Ibid.

10. Evan Allen, "Weymouth Girl Honored for Aiding Ill Mother," *Boston Globe,* March 12, 2014.

11. Twyla Tardif, "Nouns Are Not Always Learned Before Verbs: Evidence from Mandarin Speakers' Early Vocabularies," *Developmental Psychology* 32 (1996): 492–504.

12. Hiroshi Azuma, "Cross-National Research on Child Development: The Hess-Azuma Collaboration in Retrospect," in *Japanese Childrearing: Two Generations of Scholarship,* edited by David W. Schwalb and Barbara J. Schwalb (New York: Guilford Press, 1996), 234–235.

13. Misako Tsutsui Steveron, "The Mother's Role in Japanese Dinnertime Narratives" (master's thesis, University of Hawaii, Manoa, 1995), 38, cited in Takie Sugiyama Lebra, *The Japanese Self in Cultural Logic* (Honolulu: University of Hawaii Press, 2004), 76.

14. Tobin et al., *Preschool in Three Cultures Revisited,* 137.

15. George A. DeVos, "Psychocultural Continuities in Japanese Social Motivation," in Schwalb and Schwalb, *Japanese Childrearing,* 61.

16. George G. Bear, Maureen A. Manning, and Kunio Shiomi, "Children's Reasoning About Aggression: Differences Between Japan and the United States and Implications for School Discipline," *School Psychology Review* 35 (2006): 62–77, 67.

Chapter 9. Conclusions

1. Frank Furedi, *Paranoid Parenting: Abandon Your Anxieties and Be a Good Parent* (London: Allen Lane, 2001). Furedi is Emeritus Professor of Sociology at the University of Kent and a pioneer in British studies of parenting parallel to the American works cited here. Other sources from the University of Kent are Charlotte Faircloth, Diane M. Hoffman, and Linda Layne, eds., *Parenting in Global Perspective: Negotiating Ideologies of Kinship, Self, and Politics* (London: Routledge, 2013); and Ellie Lee, Jennie Bristow, Charlotte Faircloth, and Jan Macvarish, *Parenting Culture Studies* (London: Palgrave Macmillan, 2014).

2. Sharon Hays, *The Cultural Contradictions of Motherhood* (New Haven, CT: Yale University Press, 1996); Lareau, *Unequal Childhoods;* Suzanne B. Bianchi, John P. Robinson, and Melissa A. Milkie, *Changing Rhythms of American Family Life* (New York: Russell Sage Foundation, 2006); Elinor Ochs and Tamar Kremer-Sadlik, eds., *Fast-Forward Family: Home, Work, and Relationships in Middle-Class America* (Berkeley: University of California Press, 2013); Marie-Anne Suizzo, "Mother-Child Relationships in France: Balancing Autonomy and Affiliation in Everyday Interactions," *Ethos* 32 (2004): 293–323.

3. Polly Young-Eisendrath, *The Self-esteem Trap: Raising Confident and Compassionate Kids in an Age of Self-importance* (New York: Little, Brown, 2008); Leonard Sax, *The Collapse of Parenting: How We Hurt Our Kids When We Treat Them Like Grown-ups* (New York: Basic Books, 2015).

4. Senior, *All Joy and No Fun;* Druckerman, *Bringing Up Bébé.*

5. Laura Pappano, "Is Your First Grader College Ready?" *New York Times,* February 4, 2015.

6. Druckerman, *Bringing Up Bébé,* 2–3.

References

Ainsworth, Mary D. Salter, Mary C. Blehar, Everett Waters, and Sally N. Wall. 1978. *Patterns of Attachment: A Psychological Study of the Strange Situation.* Hillsdale, NJ: Erlbaum.

Azuma, Hiroshi. 1996. "Cross-National Research on Child Development: The Hess-Azuma Collaboration in Retrospect." In *Japanese Childrearing: Two Generations of Scholarship,* edited by David W. Schwalb and Barbara J. Schwalb. New York: Guilford Press.

Barnett, Homer G. 1960. *Being a Palauan.* New York: Henry Holt.

Bateson, Gregory, Don D. Jackson, Jay Haley, and John Weakland. 1956. "Toward a Theory of Schizophrenia." *Behavioral Science* 1: 251–264.

Bear, George G., Maureen A. Manning, and Kunio Shiomi. 2006. "Children's Reasoning About Aggression: Differences Between Japan and the United States and Implications for School Discipline." *School Psychology Review* 35: 62–77.

Bennett, Lynn. 1983. *Dangerous Wives and Sacred Sisters: Social and Symbolic Roles of High-Caste Women in Nepal.* New York: Columbia University Press.

Bettelheim, Bruno. 1950. *Love Is Not Enough.* Glencoe, IL: Free Press.

———. 1967. *The Empty Fortress: Infantile Autism and the Birth of the Self.* New York: Free Press.

Bianchi, Suzanne B., John P. Robinson, and Melissa A. Milkie. 2006. *Changing Rhythms of American Family Life.* New York: Russell Sage Foundation.

Biesele, Megan. 1997. "An Ideal of Unassisted Birth: Hunting, Healing, and Transformation Among the Kalahari Ju/'hoansi." In *Childbirth and Authoritative Knowledge: Cross-Cultural Perspectives,* edited by Robbie Davis-Floyd and Carolyn Sargent. Berkeley: University of California Press.

Bledsoe, Caroline, and Uche Isiugo-Abanihe. 1989. "Strategies of Child-Fosterage Among Mende Grannies in Sierra Leone." In *Reproduction* and Social Organization in Sub-Saharan Africa, edited by Ron J. Lesthaeghe. Berkeley: University of California Press.

Bolin, Inge. 2006. Growing Up in a Culture of Respect. Austin: University of Texas Press.

Bowlby, John. 1951. Maternal Care and Mental Health. Geneva: World Health Organization.

———. 1953. Child Care and the Growth of Love. Harmondsworth, UK: Penguin.

Brazelton, T. Berry. 1962. "A Child-Oriented Approach to Toilet Training." Pediatrics 29: 579–588.

Briggs, Jean. 1998. Inuit Morality Play: The Emotional Education of a Three-Year-Old. New Haven, CT: Yale University Press.

Broch, Harald. 1990. Growing Up Agreeably: Bonerate Childhood Observed. Honolulu: University of Hawaii Press.

Bronfenbrenner, Urie. 1958. "Socialization and Social Class Through Time and Space." In Readings in Social Psychology, 3rd ed., edited by Eleanor E. Maccoby, Theodore M. Newcomb, and Eugene L. Hartley. New York: Holt, Rinehart & Winston.

Cardini, Francesco, and Huang Weixin. 1998. "Moxibustion for Correction of Breech Presentation: A Randomized Controlled Trial." Journal of the American Medical Association 280: 1580–1584.

Carroll, Vern, ed. 1970. Adoption in Eastern Oceania. Honolulu: University of Hawaii Press.

Caudill, William, and David Plath. 1966. "Who Sleeps by Whom? Parent-Child Involvement in Urban Japanese Families." Psychiatry 29: 344–366.

Chisholm, James S. 1983. Navajo Infancy: An Ethological Study of Child Development. Hawthorne, NY: Aldine.

Clancy, Patricia M. 1999. "The Socialization of Affect in Japanese Mother-Child Conversation." Journal of Pragmatics 31: 1397–1421.

De Kok, Winifred. 1935. Guiding Your Child Through the Formative Years: From Birth to the Age of Five. New York: Emerson Books.

Dennis, Wayne. 1940. The Hopi Child. New York: Wiley.

DeVos, George A. 1996. "Psychocultural Continuities in Japanese Social Motivation." In Japanese Childrearing: Two Generations of Scholarship, edited by David W. Schwalb and Barbara J. Schwalb. New York: Guilford Press.

Dixon, Suzanne, Robert A. LeVine, Amy Richman, and T. Berry Brazelton. 1984. "Mother-Child Interaction Around a Teaching Task." Child Development 55: 1252–1264.

Druckerman, Pamela. 2012. *Bringing Up Bébé*. New York: Penguin Press.

Faircloth, Charlotte, Diane M. Hoffman, and Linda Layne, eds. 2013. *Parenting in Global Perspective: Negotiating Ideologies of Kinship, Self, and Politics*. London: Routledge.

Field, Tiffany. 2010. "Touch for Socio-emotional and Physical Well-being: A Review." *Developmental Review* 30: 367–383.

Fifield, Adam. 2015. *A Mighty Purpose: How Jim Grant Sold the World on Saving Its Children*. New York: Other Press.

Firth, Raymond. 1963. *We the Tikopia*. Boston: Beacon Press. (Originally published in 1936.)

Freed, Ruth S., and Stanley Freed. 1980. "Rites of Passage in Shanti Nagar." *Anthropological Papers of the American Museum of Natural History* 56: 351–353.

———. 1981. "Enculturation and Education in Shanti Nagar." *Anthropological Papers of the American Museum of Natural History* 57, part 2.

Freud, Sigmund. 1905. "Three Essays on the Theory of Sexuality." In *The Standard Edition of the Complete Psychological Works of Sigmund Freud*, vol. 7, edited by James Strachey. London: Hogarth Press, 1953.

———. 1918. "From the History of an Infantile Neurosis." In *The Standard Edition of the Complete Psychological Works of Sigmund Freud*, vol. 17, edited by James Strachey. London: Hogarth Press, 1955.

———. 1923. "The Ego and the Id." In *The Standard Edition of the Complete Psychological Works of Sigmund Freud*, vol. 19, edited by James Strachey. London: Hogarth Press, 1961.

Fromm-Reichmann, Frieda. 1948. "Notes on the Development of Treatment of Schizophrenics by Psychoanalytic Psychotherapy." *Psychiatry* 11: 263–273.

Fung, Heidi. 1999. "Becoming a Moral Child: The Socialization of Shame Among Young Chinese Children." *Ethos* 27: 180–209.

Furedi, Frank. 2001. *Paranoid Parenting: Abandon Your Anxieties and Be a Good Parent*. London: Allen Lane.

Gaskins, Suzanne. 2000. "Children's Daily Activities in a Mayan Village: A Culturally Grounded Description." *Cross-Cultural Research* 34: 375–389.

Gaskins, Suzanne, and Ruth Paradise. 2010. "Learning Through Observation in Daily Life." In *The Anthropology of Learning in Childhood*, edited by David Lancy, John Bock, and Suzanne Gaskins. Lanham, MD: Alta Mira Press.

Goldschmidt, Walter. 1976. "Absent Eyes and Idle Hands: Socialization for Low Affect Among the Sebei." In *Socialization as Cultural*

Communication: Development of a Theme in the Work of Margaret Mead, edited by Theodore Schwartz. Berkeley: University of California Press.

Goodenough, Florence L. 1931. *Anger in Young Children.* Minneapolis: University of Minnesota Press.

Gottlieb, Alma. 2007. *The Afterlife Is Where We Come From: The Culture of Infancy in West Africa.* Chicago: University of Chicago Press.

Greenfield, Patricia Marks. 2004. *Weaving Generations Together: Evolving Creativity in the Maya of Chiapas.* Santa Fe, NM: School of America Press.

Gross-Loh, Christine. 2013. *Parenting Without Borders: Surprising Lessons Parents Around the World Can Teach Us.* New York: Avery.

Grossmann, Karin, and Klaus Grossmann. 1991. "Newborn Behavior, the Quality of Early Parenting, and Later Toddler-Parent Relationships in a Group of German Infants." In *The Cultural Context of Infancy,* vol. 2, edited by J. Kevin Nugent, Barry M. Lester, and T. Berry Brazelton. Norwood, NJ: Ablex.

Grossmann, Karin, Klaus E. Grossmann, Heinz Kindler, and Peter Zimmerman. 2008. "A Wider View of Attachment and Exploration: The Influence of Mothers and Fathers on the Development of Psychological Security from Infancy to Young Adulthood." In *Handbook of Attachment,* edited by Jude Cassidy and Philip R. Shaver. New York: Guilford Press.

Grossmann, Karin, Klaus E. Grossmann, Gottfried Spangler, Gerhard Suess, and Lothar Unzner. 1985. "Maternal Sensitivity and Newborns' Orientation Responses as Related to Quality of Attachment in Northern Germany." In *Growing Points of Attachment: Theory and Research,* edited by Inge Bretherton and Everett Waters. *Monographs of the Society for Research in Child Development* (Chicago: University of Chicago Press) 50, nos. 1–2.

Gutschow, Kim. 2004. *Being a Buddhist Nun: The Struggle for Enlightenment in the Himalayas.* Cambridge, MA: Harvard University Press.

———. 2011. "From Home to Hospital: The Extension of Obstetrics in Ladakh." In *Medicine Between Science and Religion: Explorations on Tibetan Grounds,* edited by Vincanne Adams, Mona Schrempf, and Sienna Craig. London: Berghahn Press.

Harkness, Sara, and Charles M. Super. 1977. "Why African Children Are So Hard to Test." In *Issues in Cross-Cultural Research,* edited by Leonard Loeb Adler. New York: New York Academy of Sciences, 1977.

Harrington, Ann. 2012. "The Fall of the Schizophrenogenic Mother." *The Lancet* 379 (April 7): 1292–1293.

Hays, Sharon. 1996. *The Cultural Contradictions of Motherhood.* New Haven, CT: Yale University Press.

Henrich, Joseph, Steven J. Heine, and Ara Norenzayan. 2010. "The Weirdest People in the World?" *Behavioral and Brain Sciences* 33: 1–23.

Hewlett, Barry. 1991. *Intimate Fathers: The Nature and Context of Aka Pygmy Paternal Infant Care.* Ann Arbor: University of Michigan Press.

Hollan, Douglas, and Jane Wellenkamp. 1996. *The Thread of Life: Toraja Reflections on the Life Cycle.* Honolulu: University of Hawaii Press.

Holt, L. Emmett. 1914. *The Care and Feeding of Children: A Catechism for the Use of Mothers and Children's Nurses.* 7th ed. New York: D. Appleton & Co.

Hopgood, Mei-Ling. 2012. *How Eskimos Keep Their Babies Warm and Other Adventures in Parenting.* Chapel Hill, NC: Algonquin Books.

Horney, Karen. 1937. *The Neurotic Personality of Our Time.* New York: W. W. Norton.

———. 1939. *New Ways in Psychoanalysis.* New York: W. W. Norton.

———. 1950. *Neurosis and Human Growth.* New York: W. W. Norton.

Houlbrooke, Ralph A. 1984. *The English Family, 1450–1700.* London: Longman Group.

Hrdy, Sarah. 1999. *Mother Nature: A History of Mothers, Infants, and Natural Selection.* New York: Pantheon.

Hulbert, Ann. 2003. *Raising America: Experts, Parents, and a Century of Advice About Children.* New York: Random House.

Johnson, Allen. 2003. *Families of the Forest: Matsigenka Indians of the Peruvian Amazon.* Berkeley: University of California Press.

Johnston, Judith R., and M.-Y. Anita Wong. 2002. "Cultural Difference in Beliefs and Practices Concerning Talk to Children." *Journal of Speech, Language, and Hearing Research* 45: 916–926.

Jordan, Brigitte. 1993. *Birth in Four Cultures: A Crosscultural Investigation of Childbirth in Yucatan, Holland, Sweden, and the United States.* 4th ed. Long Grove, IL: Waveland Press.

Kagan, Jerome. 2013. *The Human Spark: The Science of Human Development.* New York: Basic Books.

Kartner, Joscha, Heidi Keller, and Relendis Yovsi. 2010. "Mother-Infant Interaction During the First 3 Months: The Emergence of Culture-Specific Contingency Patterns." *Child Development* 81: 540–554.

Keller, Heidi. 2007. *Cultures of Infancy.* Mahwah, NJ: Erlbaum.

Kenyatta, Jomo. 1962. *Facing Mount Kenya.* New York: Vintage Books. (Originally published in 1938.)

Kertzer, David. 1993. *Sacrificed for Honor: Italian Infant Abandonment and the Politics of Reproductive Control.* Boston: Beacon Press.

Kobayashi, Shusuke. 2001. "Japanese Mother-Child Relationships: Skill Acquisition Before the Preschool Years." In *Japanese Frames of Mind: Cultural Perspectives on Human Development,* edited by Hidetada Shimizu and Robert A. LeVine. New York: Cambridge University Press.

Kohut, Heinz. 1971. *The Analysis of the Self.* New York: International Universities Press.

Konner, Melvin J. 1972. "Aspects of the Developmental Ethology of a Foraging People." In *Ethological Studies of Child Behavior,* edited by Nicholas Blurton-Jones. Cambridge: Cambridge University Press.

———. 1975. "Relations Among Infants and Juveniles in Comparative Perspective." In *Friendship and Peer Relations,* edited by Michael Lewis and Leonard A. Rosenblum. New York: Wiley.

Kussmaul, Ann. 1981. *Servants in Husbandry in Early Modern England.* Cambridge: Cambridge University Press.

Lancy, David. 1996. *Playing on the Mother-Ground: Cultural Routines for Children's Development.* New York: Guilford Press.

———. 2008. *The Anthropology of Childhood: Cherubs, Chattel, Changelings.* New York: Cambridge University Press.

Lareau, Annette. 2003. *Unequal Childhoods: Class, Race, and Family Life.* Berkeley: University of California Press.

Larsen, Ulla. 1989. "A Comparative Study of the Levels and the Differentials of Sterility in Cameroon, Kenya, and Sudan." In *Reproduction and Social Organization in Sub-Saharan Africa,* edited by Ron J. Lesthaeghe. Berkeley: University of California Press.

Lave, Jean, and Etienne Wenger. 1991. *Situated Learning: Legitimate Peripheral Participation.* Cambridge: Cambridge University Press.

LeBillon, Karen. 2012. *French Kids Eat Everything.* New York: HarperCollins.

Lebra, Takie Sugiyama. 2004. *The Japanese Self in Cultural Logic.* Honolulu: University of Hawaii Press.

Lee, Ellie, Jennie Bristow, Charlotte Faircloth, and Jan Macvarish, eds. 2014. *Parenting Culture Studies.* London: Palgrave Macmillan.

LePore, Jill. 2009. "Baby Food." *The New Yorker,* January 19.

Levenstein, Harvey. 1983. "'Best for Babies' or 'Preventable Infanticide'? The Controversy over Artificial Feeding of Infants in America, 1880–1920." *Journal of American History* 70: 75–94.

LeVine, Robert A. 2004. "Challenging Expert Knowledge: Findings from an African Study of Infant Care and Development." In *Childhood and Adolescence: Cross-Cultural Perspectives and Applications,* edited by Uwe Gielen and Jaipaul Roopnarine. Westport, CT: Praeger.

LeVine, Robert A., Suzanne Dixon, Sarah LeVine, Amy Richman, P. Herbert Leiderman, and T. Berry Brazelton. 1994. *Child Care and Culture: Lessons from Africa.* New York: Cambridge University Press.

LeVine, Robert A., Sarah LeVine, Beatrice Schnell-Anzola, Meredith Rowe, and Emily Dexter. 2012. *Literacy and Mothering: How Women's Schooling Changes the Lives of the World's Children.* New York: Oxford University Press.

LeVine, Robert A., and Barbara B. Lloyd. 1966. *Nyansongo: A Gusii Community in Kenya.* New York: Wiley.

LeVine, Sarah. 1979. *Mothers and Wives: Gusii Women of East Africa.* Chicago: University of Chicago Press.

Li, Jin. 2012. *Cultural Foundations of Learning: East and West.* New York: Cambridge University Press.

Lipset, David. 1980. *Gregory Bateson: The Legacy of a Scientist.* Englewood Cliffs, NJ: Prentice-Hall.

Macfarlane, Alan. 1978. *The Origins of English Individualism: The Family, Property and Social Transition.* New York: Cambridge University Press.

Macfarlane, Jean Walker, Lucile Allen, and Marjorie P. Honzik. 1954. *A Developmental Study of the Behavior Problems of Normal Children Between 21 Months and 14 Years.* Berkeley: University of California Press.

Mageo, Jeanette M. 2013. "Toward a Cultural Psychodynamics of Attachment: Samoa and US Comparisons." In *Attachment Reconsidered: Cultural Perspectives on a Western Theory,* edited by Naomi Quinn and Jeanette M. Mageo. New York: Palgrave Macmillan.

Mahler, Margaret, Fred Pine, and Anni Bergmann. 1975. *The Psychological Birth of the Human Infant.* New York: Basic Books.

Malinowski, Bronislaw. 1929. *The Sexual Life of Savages in North-Western Melanesia.* London: George Routledge & Sons.

Mann, Horace. 1846. *Report of an Educational Tour in Germany and Parts of Great Britain and Ireland.* London: Simpkin, Marshall & Co.

Martin, John A., David R. King, Eleanor E. Maccoby, and Carol Nagy Jacklin. 1984. "Secular Trends and Individual Differences in Toilet-Training Progress." *Journal of Pediatric Psychology* 9: 457–467.

Martini, Mary, and John Kirkpatrick. 1992. "Parenting in Polynesia: A View from the Marquesas." In *Parent-Child Socialization in Diverse*

Cultures, edited by Jaipaul L. Roopnarine and Bruce Carter, vol. 5 of *Annual Advances in Applied Developmental Psychology.* Norwood, NJ: Ablex.

Marvin, Robert S., Thomas L. VanDevender, Margaret I. Iwanaga, Sarah LeVine, and Robert A. LeVine. 1977. "Infant-Caregiver Attachment Among the Hausa of Nigeria." In *Ecological Factors in Human Development,* edited by Harry McGurk. Amsterdam: North-Holland Publishing.

Maynard, Ashley. 2002. "Cultural Teaching: The Development of Teaching Skills in Maya Sibling Interactions." *Child Development* 73: 969–982.

McKenna, James, and Lee Gettler. 2016. "There Is No Such Thing as Infant Sleep, There Is No Such Thing as Breast-feeding, There Is Only Breastsleeping." *Acta Paediatrica* 105: 17–21.

Mead, Margaret. 1928. *Coming of Age in Samoa.* New York: William Morrow.

———. 1930. *Growing Up in New Guinea.* New York: William Morrow.

Miller, Peggy J., Todd L. Sandel, Chung-Hui Liang, and Heidi Fung. "Narrating Transgressions in Longwood: The Discourses, Meanings, and Paradoxes of an American Socializing Practice." *Ethos* 29, no. 2 (2001): 159–186.

Mintz, Steven. 2004. *Huck's Raft: A History of American Childhood.* Cambridge, MA: Harvard University Press.

Newson, John, and Elizabeth Newson. 1963. *Patterns of Infant Care in an Urban Community.* Harmondsworth, UK: Penguin Books.

———. 1968. *Four Years Old in an Urban Community.* London: George Allen & Unwin.

NICHD Early Child Care Research Network. "The Effects of Infant Child Care on Infant-Mother Attachment Security: Results of the NICHD Study of Early Child Care." *Child Development* 68, no. 5 (1997): 860–879.

Obeyesekere, Gananath. 1963. "Pregnancy Cravings (Dola-Duka) in Relation to Social Structure and Personality in a Sinhalese Village." *American Anthropologist* 65 (1963): 323–342.

Ochs, Elinor, and Carolina Izquierdo. 2009. "Responsibility in Childhood: Three Developmental Trajectories." *Ethos* 37: 391–402.

Ochs, Elinor, and Tamar Kremer-Sadlik, eds. 2013. *Fast-Forward Family: Home, Work, and Relationships in Middle-Class America.* Berkeley: University of California Press.

Okami, Paul. 1995. "Childhood Exposure to Parental Nudity, Parent-Child Co-sleeping, and 'Primal Scenes': A Review of Clinical Opinion and Empirical Evidence." *Journal of Sex Research* 32: 51–64.

———. 1998. "Early Childhood Exposure to Parental Nudity and Scenes of Parental Sexuality ('Primal Scenes'): An 18-Year Longitudinal Study of Outcome." *Archives of Sexual Behavior* 27: 361–384.

Otto, Hiltrud, and Heidi Keller, eds. 2014. *Different Faces of Attachment: Cultural Variations on a Universal Human Need.* Cambridge: Cambridge University Press.

Paradise, Ruth, and Barbara Rogoff. 2009. "Side by Side: Learning by Observing and Pitching In." *Ethos* 37: 102–138.

Perry, Helen Swick. 1982. *Psychiatrist of America: The Life of Harry Stack Sullivan.* Cambridge, MA: Harvard University Press.

Potegal, Michael, Michael R. Kosorok, and Richard J. Davidson. 2003. "Temper Tantrums in Young Children: 1. Behavioral Composition." *Journal of Developmental and Behavioral Pediatrics* 24: 140–147.

———. 2003. "Temper Tantrums in Young Children: 2. Tantrum Duration and Temporal Organization." *Journal of Developmental and Behavioral Pediatrics* 24: 148.

Quinn, Naomi, and Jeanette Mageo, eds. 2013. *Attachment Reconsidered: Cultural Perspectives on a Western Theory.* New York: Palgrave Macmillan.

Richman, Amy, Patrice M. Miller, and Robert A. LeVine. 1992. "Cultural and Educational Variations in Maternal Responsiveness." *Developmental Psychology* 28: 614–621.

Rogoff, Barbara. 1990. *Apprenticeship in Thinking: Cognitive Development in Social Context.* New York: Oxford University Press.

———. 2011. *Developing Destinies: A Mayan Midwife and Town.* New York: Oxford University Press.

Rogoff, Barbara, Jayanthi Mistry, Artin Göncü, Christine Mosier, Pablo Chavajay, and Shirley Brice Health. 1993. "Guided Participation in Cultural Activity by Toddlers and Caregivers." *Monographs of the Society for Research in Child Development* 58, serial no. 236 (1993).

Röttger-Rössler, Birgitt. 2014. "Bonding and Belonging Beyond WEIRD Worlds: Re-thinking Attachment Theory on the Basis of Cross-cultural Anthropological Data." In *Different Faces of Attachment: Cultural Variations on a Universal Human Need,* edited by Hiltrud Otto and Heidi Keller. Cambridge: Cambridge University Press.

Sameroff, Arnold, and Marshall Haith, eds. 1996. *The Five to Seven Year Shift: The Age of Reason and Responsibility.* Chicago: University of Chicago Press.

Sax, Leonard. 2015. *The Collapse of Parenting: How We Hurt Our Kids When We Treat Them Like Grown-ups.* New York: Basic Books.

Schieffelin, Bambi. 1990. *The Give and Take of Everyday Life: Language Socialization of Kaluli Children.* Cambridge: Cambridge University Press.

Schieffelin, Bambi, and Elinor Ochs, eds. 1986. *Language Socialization Across Cultures.* Cambridge: Cambridge University Press.

Sears, Robert R., Eleanor E. Maccoby, and Harry Levin. 1957. *Patterns of Child Rearing.* New York: Harper & Row.

Senior, Jennifer. 2014. *All Joy and No Fun: The Paradox of Modern Parenthood.* New York: Ecco.

Seymour, Susan. 1988. "Expressions of Responsibility Among Indian Children: Some Precursors of Adult Status and Sex Roles." *Ethos* 16: 355–370.

———. 1999. *Women, Family, and Child Care in India: A World in Transition.* New York: Cambridge University Press.

Sharma, Dinesh, and Robert A. LeVine. 1998. "Child Care in India: A Comparative Developmental View of Infant Social Environments." In *Socioemotional Development Across Cultures,* edited by Dinesh Sharma and Kurt Fischer. New Directions for Child Development 81. San Francisco: Jossey-Bass.

Shostak, Marjorie. 1981. *Nisa: The Life and Words of a !Kung Woman.* Cambridge, MA: Harvard University Press.

Shweder, Richard A., Lene Jensen, and William Goldstein. 1995. "Who Sleeps By Whom Revisited: A Method for Extracting the Moral 'Goods' Implicit in Praxis." In *Cultural Practices as Context for Development,* vol. 67, *New Directions for Child Development,* edited by Jacqueline Goodnow, Peggy Miller, and Frank Kessel. San Francisco: Jossey-Bass.

Spock, Benjamin. 1946. *The Common Sense Book of Baby and Child Care.* New York: Duell, Sloan and Pearce.

Stafford, Charles. 1995. *The Roads of Chinese Childhood: Learning and Identification in Angang.* New York: Cambridge University Press.

Starr, Paul. 1982. *The Social Transformation of American Medicine.* New York: Basic Books.

Stendler, Celia B. 1950. "Sixty Years of Child Training Practices: Revolution in the Nursery." *Journal of Pediatrics* 36: 122–134.

Steveron, Misako Tsutsui. 1995. "The Mother's Role in Japanese Dinnertime Narratives." Master's thesis, University of Hawaii, Manoa.

Straus, Murray A. 2009. "Corporal Punishment." In *The Child: An Encyclopedic Companion,* edited by Richard A. Shweder. Chicago: University of Chicago Press.

Suizzo, Marie-Anne. 2004. "Mother-Child Relationships in France: Balancing Autonomy and Affiliation in Everyday Interactions." *Ethos* 32: 293–323.

Sullivan, Harry Stack. 1940. *Conceptions of Modern Psychiatry.* New York: W. W. Norton.

Tardif, Twyla. 1996. "Nouns Are Not Always Learned Before Verbs: Evidence from Mandarin Speakers' Early Vocabularies." *Developmental Psychology* 32: 492–504.

Task Force on Sudden Infant Death Syndrome. 2011. "SIDS and Other Sleep-Related Infant Deaths: Expansion of Recommendations for a Safe Infant Sleeping Environment." *Pediatrics* 128: e1341–e1367.

Tobin, Joseph, Yeh Hsueh, and Mayumi Karasawa. 2009. *Preschool in Three Cultures Revisited: China, Japan, and the United States.* Chicago: University of Chicago Press.

Tronick, Edward Z., Gilda Morelli, and Steve Winn. 1987. "Multiple Caretaking of Efe (Pygmy) Infants." *American Anthropologist* 89: 96–106.

United Nations Department of Economic and Social Affairs, Population Division, 2012, *World Population Prospects: The 2012 Revision: Volume 1, Highlights and Advance Tables.*

United Nations Secretary-General's Office. 2015. *The Millennium Goals Report 2015.* Available at: http://www.un.org/millenniumgoals/2015 _MDG_Report/pdf/MDG%202015%20rev%20(July%201).pdf.

US Department of Health and Human Services. Centers for Disease Control and Prevention (CDC). "Breastfeeding Report Card—United States, 2011." Available at: http://www.cdc.gov/breastfeeding/pdf/2011breast feedingreportcard.pdf.

Vicedo, Marga. 2013. *The Nature and Nurture of Love: From Imprinting to Attachment in Cold War America.* Chicago: University of Chicago Press.

Watson, John B. 1928. *Psychological Care of Infant and Child.* New York: W. W. Norton.

Watson-Gegeo, Karen. 2001. "Fantasy and Reality: The Dialectic of Work and Play in Kwara'ae Children's Lives." *Ethos* 29: 138–158.

Weiner, Myron. 1991. *The Child and the State in India: Child Labor and Education Policy in Comparative Perspective.* Princeton, NJ: Princeton University Press.

Weisner, Thomas S. 2005. "Attachment as a Cultural and Ecological Problem with Pluralistic Solutions." *Human Development* 48: 89–94.

Whiting, John W. M. 1993. "Environmental Constraints on Infant Care Practices." In *Culture and Human Development: The Selected Papers of John Whiting,* edited by Eleanor C. Chasdi. New York: Cambridge University Press.

Winnicott, D. W. 1957. *The Child and the Family: First Relationships.* London: Tavistock.

Yarrow, Marian R., John D. Campbell, and Roger V. Burton. 1968. *Child Rearing: An Inquiry into Research and Methods.* San Francisco: Jossey-Bass.

Young-Eisendrath, Polly. 2008. *The Self-esteem Trap: Raising Confident and Compassionate Kids in an Age of Self-importance.* New York: Little, Brown.

Yovsi, Relendis, Joscha Kartner, Heidi Keller, and A. Lohaus. 2009. "Maternal Interactional Quality in Two Cultural Environments." *Journal of Cross-Cultural Psychology* 40: 701–707.

Index

agrarian societies (*continued*)
  parents helping speech
    development in toddlers,
    114–115
  pathways for child development,
    187–188
  precocious children, 169–170,
    179
  sharing infant care in joint
    families, 95–98
  sibling harmony, 112–114
  siblings sharing infant care,
    98–99
  task assignment in toddlers,
    133–136
  temper tantrums in toddlers,
    130–133
  toilet training in China and
    India, 122–125
  variability in social conditions,
    xix–xx
  variations in human parenting,
    185
  See also Gusii people; Hausa
    people; Mayan people
Ainsworth, Mary, 24, 170–171
Aka people, xviii, 79, 99
animal husbandry, xi, xii–xiv
anxiety over parenting, 182–184
apprenticeships, xx, 74, 100–101,
    117–118, 139–140,
    148–151
attachment theory
  infant attachment, 23–27
  self-reliance in children,
    171–172
  skin-to-skin versus face-to-face
    interaction, 83–84
autism, 19–23
Azuma, Hiroshi, 177

Baby and Child Care (Spock), 13,
    15
Baltimore study, 170–173
Barnett, Homer, 130–133
Bateson, Gregory, 19
begging children, 150
behavior
  Holt's moral mandate disguised
    as scientific parenting, 5–8
  tantrums, 126–133
  See also precocious children
behaviorism, 8–9
Beng people
  attachment theory, 24–25
  breast-feeding other women's
    children, 92
  hierarchical routines, 80
  toddlers' speech development,
    117
Bettelheim, Bruno, 12, 20–23
Bielefeld study, 170–173
bilingual development, 176
birth. *See* pregnancy and birth
Bledsoe, Caroline, 100–101
bond-friends, 101
Botswana: breech presentation in
    birth, 39
bottle-feeding, 51–57
Bowlby, John, 16–19, 22, 26
Bowlby-Ainsworth model, 24–27,
    83
Brazelton, T. Berry, 62, 122, 124
breast-feeding
  American views on, 51–57
  as social interaction, 74–75
  attachment theory, 24–25
  cultural priorities and
    differences, 51–59
  Hausa customs, x
  in sub-Saharan Africa, 57–59

Robert A. LeVine and **Sarah LeVine** have collaborated for forty-seven years and have written two previous books together, *Child Care and Culture* and *Literacy and Mothering*. Robert is the Roy E. Larsen Professor of Education and Human Development Emeritus at Harvard University. Sarah is an anthropologist who has conducted research on four continents and coordinated the fieldwork of Harvard's Project on Maternal Schooling. Her books include *Dolor y Alegría, Mothers and Wives,* and *The Saint of Kathmandu.*